DIRECTORS

Responsibilities and liabilities

DIRECTORS

Responsibilities and liabilities

Fifth edition

Peter Souster

Baker Tilly

Croner.CCH Group Ltd
145 London Road
Kingston upon Thames
Surrey KT2 6SR
Tel: 020 8247 1262
Fax: 020 8547 2637
E-mail: bookcomp@croner.cch.co.uk
www.croner.co.uk

ISBN 1 84140 235 4

First edition published 1986 as *The Responsible Director*.
Revised 1987.
Second edition published 1990 as *Directors' Responsibilities and Liabilities* (ISBN 1 85355 097 3).
Third edition published 1993 (ISBN 1 85355 415 4).
Fourth edition published 1998.
Fifth edition published 2002.

The law is stated as at 1 July 2002.

British Library Cataloguing-in-Publication Data.

A catalogue record for this book is available from the British Library.

Throughout this book the male pronoun has been used with reference to both the male and the female.

Typeset by J&L Composition, Filey, North Yorkshire
Printed by Bell & Bain, Glasgow

Acknowledgements

I am very grateful to the directors and proprietors of so many smaller companies who are 'at the sharp end' and who have shared their experiences and problems with me. This book is written with their interest very much in mind in the hope that it will help prospective directors in particular, appreciate more fully the obligations they are about to assume.

I must acknowledge the very clear analysis of directors' duties contained in articles written in the *Company Lawyer* (published by Sweet & Maxwell) by Alan Walters, lecturer in corporate law at Nottingham Trent University, as well as the help given by Mrs Valerie Fogleman of Barlow Lyde and Gilbert on environmental law issues.

I also would like to thank my colleagues at Baker Tilly for their encouragement, particularly John Hudson and his team for their guidance on technical issues and Clare Lewin for her patience in struggling to interpret my scrawl through numerous drafts. However, none of this would have been possible without the continued support of my long suffering wife Anna.

Peter Souster
Baker Tilly
2 Bloomsbury Street
London
WC1B 3ST

September 2002

Acknowledgements

Contents

"It is of the greatest importance that any individual who undertakes the statutory and fiduciary obligations of being a company director should realise that these are inescapable personal responsibilities."

"Lord Woolf M.R. in the Court of Appeal – SSTI v Griffiths & Ors Re: Westwid Packing Services Ltd (No 3) [1998] BCC 836"

Introduction

This book aims to highlight the main areas of essential knowledge with which directors of all companies, of whatever size, should be familiar. Managing company affairs in accordance with the requirements of the Companies Acts 1985 and 1989 requires directors to have, and to exercise, administrative and financial skills, many of which cannot be delegated. The Insolvency Act 1986 and the Company Directors Disqualification Act 1986 imposed more severe sanctions against directors who act irresponsibly or fail to exercise adequately their duties to the company, shareholders, creditors and outsiders.

Since 1986, the decisions of the Courts have made it clear that all directors are expected to have a reasonable understanding of their legal responsibilities and of their company's accounting obligations. A higher level of skill and competence is now expected from directors, particularly those who are professionally qualified; and those who do not fulfil their obligations, even through inaction, can find themselves to be held to account for their failings. The Courts will now use the legislation to enable redress to be obtained from directors personally, as well as from the company they control. For example, in certain circumstances directors can be asked to pay for the cost of a clean-up operation where there have been negligent breaches of environmental legislation or make a contribution towards creditors' losses should their company fail and go into liquidation.

The number of directors disqualified because they were found to be unfit to be involved in the management of a company has increased every year since 1994. The primary objectives of disqualification are, first, to protect the public against the conduct of those who are regarded by the Court as a danger to creditors and other third parties with whom they deal; and second, to encourage other directors to behave well.

In America the spectacular collapses this summer of Enron Corporation and WorldCom have focused attention of government and the regulators on the activities and responsibilities of both directors and auditors. A Senate committee delivered a damning report on the Enron debacle, accusing the energy group's directors of lying when they claimed they knew nothing of the gathering financial disaster. There was scathing criticism of the Enron directors for awarding themselves bonuses for 2000 which represented more than 75 per cent of the group's reported net income for the year. A Senate permanent sub-committee is reported as saying 'Apparently, no-one on the board ever added up the numbers.' This has strengthened the political determination to make Boards of directors accountable for their companies' transgressions to such an extent that the United States is seeking to make the directors of UK companies, which are controlled from the United States subject to US regulation.

The impact of these financial scandals was immediate – around the world, stock markets dived as investors' confidence in the way major companies were being run was badly shaken. In the United Kingdom we experienced similar shocks, albeit on a smaller scale, during the excesses of the 1980s and the recession of the early 1990s. Corporate Governance – the system by which companies are directed and controlled – has been regularly reviewed since 1991 both by the regulatory authorities and the responsible business community. As a consequence, many believe our regulatory regime is now more developed than in the United States, albeit that the Combined Code is a form of voluntary regulation, with no statutory backing. However, to be effective, any process of regulation must respond quickly to a changing market place and adapt to meet changing expectations.

Following Enron, the theme of much of the current debate is how to strengthen the role of board directors, and no doubt the report of the Higgs' committee set up by the UK Government in the summer of 2002 to review the role and effectiveness of non-executive directors will contribute to this discussion.

During the last 10 years the myriad of legislation impacting upon companies in the UK and the businesses operated by them has grown enormously, either on the back of inconsistent case law, or in accordance with the requirements of European Directives. Changes in the law have frequently been grafted onto the existing legislation in response to a particular issue of the day, with the consequence that the legislation lacks coherence and is difficult to understand. Therefore, in early 1998, the Government launched a wide-ranging review of company law with the objective of establishing a legal framework which promotes consistency and transparency in the law, whilst at the same time promoting the competitiveness of British companies and facilitating effective wealth creation, in the widest sense.

The review was led by an independent Steering Group, whose final report was published in July 2001. They considered the role of a director to be at the heart of company law and recommended that directors' duties should be codified by statute in order to provide clear and accessible guidance for directors. In July 2002 the Government published a consultative White Paper which broadly endorses the Review Group's approach.

The proposals for change are extensive and, if substantially implemented, they will have a significant impact upon the ways in which companies conduct their affairs. It should also clarify the particular responsibilities of directors both to shareholders, and to those parties with whom the company either deals, or who are affected by the company's activities.

The other major piece of legislation which is also expected to become law during 2003 is the Enterprise Bill. Comments have been included on those parts of the Bill dealing with Corporate Insolvency procedures. In view of the significance of the proposed changes likely to result from these two substantial pieces of new legislation, an outline of the key elements has been included in so far as they affect the responsibilities of directors. Obviously amendments will be made during their passage through Parliament before the current proposals become law, but it is expected that the principal thrust of each bill will remain unchanged. In all other respects, this book is written on the basis of the law as it stands as at 1 July 2002.

Readers should not rely upon this book as a comprehensive guide to the legislation, but it is hoped it will prove an *aide-mémoire* for directors, particularly of private companies. It is not a substitute for professional advice, because each situation is individual and requires specific solutions. The obligations and responsibilities of all directors have undoubtedly become much more onerous since this book was first written in 1986, but I hope this edition will continue to forewarn and forearm directors against the pitfalls they should expect to encounter. With timely information, proper advice and effective action, directors can still minimise the problems they face and maximise the opportunities before them.

Peter Souster
September 2002

1 Companies

The entrepreneur has a choice: to trade alone, to join up with partners, or to trade as a limited company.

The sole trader and general partnership run their own show, putting in their skill and their money and taking out the profits, but they are also responsible for all business losses, debts and obligations.

1.1 Why a company?

Incorporating business activities into a company confers life on the business as a separate legal person; profits and losses are the company's and it has its own debts and obligations. The business continues in spite of the resignation, bankruptcy or death of directors and shareholders – events which would put the sole trader out of business or lead to dissolution of a partnership. The shareholders, the company members – who may also be directors – own the company. Profits can be taken out as income by way of dividend or payment for services rendered or even capitalised by way of a bonus issue of shares. Directors' liability for company debts and obligations is, unless they or the company act beyond their powers, or there is negligence, recklessness or fraud, limited to the nominal (that is, face or par) value of their shareholding; if shares are paid for in full (fully paid up) there is no further liability, even if the business becomes insolvent.

A company is often recommended as the ideal vehicle for expansion: additional shareholders and participants, further capital and loans, can be readily assimilated into the corporate structure and corporate share ownership ensures continuity, but the shareholders owning the majority are able to rule the business and can usually retain tight control of company affairs.

1.1.1 What sort of company?

The vast majority of companies are private companies limited by shares, that is, private limited companies. Of the 1,526,454 registered, active companies listed on the Companies Register at the end of July 2002, only just under one per cent of these were public companies – public limited companies or plcs – with the required minimum nominal value of allotted share capital of £50,000. The nominal value of each share must be at least 25 per cent paid up. The limited company, private or public, takes on its own debts and obligations and ownership of the company is separated from liability.

1.2 Incorporation

A company is formed by registering it with the Registrar of Companies at Companies House, filing details of the directors, the company secretary and the company's constitution – that is, its memorandum of association and articles of association – and paying the appropriate fee.

1.2.1 Formation

Most trading operations can operate through a ready-made 'off the shelf' company, which is already registered at Companies House and can be acquired through most firms of accountants or solicitors, or bought directly from one of the main registration agents who advertise in professional and financial journals. All the necessary documentation will have been filed with the Registrar and the company will have a Certificate of Incorporation, without which it cannot start trading.

The existing shareholders, directors and company secretary then resign in favour of the required nominees. The name and main objects clause of the memorandum can be changed but it should be ensured that the existing principal objects clause covers the main business activities. However, this process has been simplified for companies incorporated after the Companies Act 1989 which permits a company's principal object to be that of 'a general commercial company'.

The procedure is relatively straightforward and inexpensive, although starting from scratch can involve some additional delays. There are, however, technicalities and you should seek professional advice before shopping for a company, particularly if you trade in a specialised field. Care should be taken to ensure that the company has not traded before and has no contingent liabilities.

1.2.2 Publicity

Incorporation brings a certain amount of publicity: accounts, reports and other company information must be filed at Companies House where they are open to public inspection. The company and its officers must comply with company legislation, which imposes more stringent obligations on public companies. You can register a company with unlimited liability in which case accounts and reports are not filed but this and other statutory concessions expose shareholders to full liability for company debts and obligations.

1.2.3 Company names

You can use a ready-made company's name or choose another – which may be your existing business name – after incorporation, with the appropriate addition to show limited, private or public liability. The chosen name has to be approved by the Registrar. It may be rejected if, for any reason, it is considered to be too similar to that of another company, or its use would constitute a criminal offence, is offensive or misleading. The short list of names requiring the approval of the Secretary of State changes from time to time and the Secretary can require a change of name to ensure compliance with the legislation.

The company's name must be clearly shown on all business correspondence and documentation, including cheques and other negotiable instruments, order forms, invoices and the company seal, and be displayed prominently at any premises where the company operates. If any of the directors' names are included on business letters and order forms, then the names of all directors must be stated; the company's registered number and the address of the registered office must also be shown. Company seals are no longer a legal necessity, and any document executed by the company has the same effect as one executed under seal, providing it is signed by either two directors or one director and the company secretary.

Anyone with whom you do or discuss business but who does not visit the premises must be given these written details. Non-compliance with any of the requirements is an offence for which the company or its officers may be fined and, if the company name is not on negotiable instruments or purchase orders are not placed in its registered name, the directors may be personally liable if payment is not made by the company.

1.2.4 Assets and liabilities

It is important that a formal transfer agreement is executed transferring existing assets and liabilities to the company upon incorporation, and professional advice should be sought as to the tax and legal aspects of the transfer before the agreement is finalised. Profits can only be made from the sale of assets to the company with the consent of the company – that is, the consent of the shareholders in general meeting – after full disclosure of the details of the transaction. If there is non-disclosure or the sale is not at a fair market value, the company can set it aside.

1.3 Advantages and disadvantages of incorporation

The cost of the advantages of limited liability and, for public companies, of the greater marketability for shares, is a heavier burden of disclosure and accountability. The Companies Act 1985, as amended by the Insolvency Act 1986 and the Companies Act 1989, currently governs their conduct and administration. The principal purpose of this legislation is to protect third parties – creditors, customers and employees – as well as shareholders and investors. The excesses of the 1980's and the difficulties of the 1990s led to the publication of reports on the disclosure of directors' remuneration and on corporate governance issues – the Cadbury, Greenbury and Hempel reports. In June 1998 these were consolidated into The Combined Code with which all fully listed companies are expected to comply. The Code brings into focus much more sharply the previously implied responsibilities of all directors, particularly with regard to the role of the non-executive director.

1.3.1 Finance

When a sole trader or partnership borrows money, the contingent liability of the proprietor, that is, their personal liability for business debts, is increased accordingly. However, when a company raises additional loan finance or working capital the shareholders', i.e., the owners', personal liability does not change. Additional shareholders are, in effect, subscribing for a share of existing and future profits but their claim is against the company only, not the directors and other shareholders. Equity capital can be raised by special share issues, giving preferential rights to dividends or the return of their share capital, with, perhaps, restricted voting rights to ensure retention of control by the original shareholders.

In addition, a company can borrow on the security of a floating charge, which permits the company to deal with assets, such as stock in trade, even though they have been charged as security to raise working capital. In addition there has been a dramatic growth in lending secured on specific assets, including invoice discounting and stock finance, which has replaced in part anyway, the more traditional bank overdraft source of finance. There are also tax advantages for the investor under the Enterprise Investment Scheme which only applies to investments in qualifying companies. Banks often prefer customers to be protected by limited liability, albeit supported by personal guarantees, and suppliers usually prefer to deal with a limited company, as they have access to information at Companies House.

1.3.2 Tax

Sole traders and partnerships pay income tax. Sole traders' and partners' business profits are taxed as their income, irrespective of how much they leave in the business as working capital. Under self-assessment, each partner is solely responsible for the tax on his or her share of the firm's profits.

A partner (but not a sole trader) can receive interest on a loan to the business, but he pays income tax on that interest. The same is true of a director who makes a loan to a company.

Directors pay income tax on their remuneration, and also on any benefits in kind or dividend income received. The company must by law operate PAYE on cash remuneration, and all benefits and expenses must be notified by the company to the Inland Revenue annually on a P11D form. Benefits and expenses taken by a sole trader or partner do not require a P11D, but must be taken into account when computing the taxable profits of the business.

Under self-assessment, sole traders and partners generally pay most of their income tax in two equal instalments, on 31 January in the tax year and six months later on the following 31 July. Company directors, on the other hand, usually pay most of their tax through the PAYE system, and do not generally have to make payments on account. This can give the director greater control over the timing of tax payments.

A partner or sole trader can draw funds from the business without restriction, and without a tax charge, whereas, subject to certain limited exceptions, it is illegal for a company to provide loans or credit facilities to a director. If a loan is made, this can lead to tax charges on the director and the company.

A company pays corporation tax on its profits for the accounting period. At current rates of tax (2001/02), company profits are usually subject to corporation tax at a lower rate than the income tax charge on similar profits of an unincorporated business. However, if any of the company's profits are withdrawn, either as remuneration or by way of dividend, the tax saving may be reduced, and the total liability for the company may even be increased because of the effect of National Insurance contributions payable on salaries.

Large companies, i.e., those with taxable profits in excess of £1.5 million have to pay part or all of their corporation tax in advance, by quarterly instalments. The monetary limit is divided among all the companies in the group or under the same common control, so that such companies may have to make quarterly payments at a lower level of taxable profits.

The main aspects of tax to consider are set out on the table on pages 10–11, but it is essential to obtain expert professional advice to ensure that maximum advantages are derived both in respect of current income and the future needs of the proprietors and the business.

***Table 1:* The basis of taxation for unincorporated traders, directors and companies (as from 1.4.02)**
Some details may be affected by subsequent legislation, and in particular by the Finance Act 2002

Detail	*Sole Trader or Partnership*	*Director*	*Company*
Status	Self-employed	Employee	Separate Entity
Tax on trading profits			
Rate	Income Tax – Schedule D 10%–40%	Income Tax – Schedule E 10%–40%	Corporation Tax 10%–30%
Profits assessed	Current year normally	Fiscal year – receipts basis	Accounting year – actual
Payment date	31 January and 31 July	During the year through PAYE	Currently 9 months after the year end, quarterly for large companies
Working spouse	Generally share in profits if a partner	During the year through PAYE	Salary to be commensurate with work undertaken
Overseas earnings	Probably fully assessable	Normally fully assessable	Taxable
Pension contributions	Premiums for personal pensions are restricted to a percentage of relevant earnings – 17.5%–40% depending on age	Contributions restricted to 15% of remuneration	All contributions generally tax deductible (although relief may be spread when abnormal contributions are made)
Interest on borrowings	Tax deductible, subject to restrictions	Interest on loans to company; tax deductible in certain circumstances	Generally a tax deductible expense or charge against profits
National Insurance	Class 2 – £2.00 per week; Class 4 – 7% of profits, Maximum £1,806.35 p.a.	Class 1 – maximum £2,579.20 p.a.	Class 1 and 1A – up to 11.8% on director's remuneration and benefits; tax deductible

Capital gains tax			
Rate	10%–40%, subject to annual exemption and taper relief	10%–40%, subject to annual exemption and taper relief	Taxed as other profits at 0–30% after indexation
Retirement relief (to be phased out by 5 April 2003)	If aged 50 or more and owned business for at least 1 year	If full-time working employee owning 5% or more of the company's shares	N/A

The effect of trading losses and the impact of inheritance tax have not been considered.

1.3.3 Retirement benefits

Approved company pension schemes may provide better benefits than those paid under personal pension plans or retirement annuity contracts used by the self-employed and those in non-pensionable employment. The level of tax deductible premium that both the self-employed and directors can pay is restricted but there is no limit on the overall contributions paid by a company for its directors in respect of a company scheme, although there is a limit on the benefits that can ultimately be paid to a director imposed by the Inland Revenue Pension Schemes Office.

Retirement benefits for directors and employees depend on contributions paid and accumulated, and often single contributions can be made from time to time to increase the benefits derived from the fixed annual contribution. How far this is possible will depend on the company's level of profits and the individual's need for immediate personal income, as opposed to increased retirement benefit, but the company's pension contribution to an approved scheme is not regarded, at present, as remuneration for the purposes of fixing National Insurance contributions.

1.3.4 National Insurance contributions

The company's (employer's) contributions currently payable for directors are significantly more than those paid by the owner of an unincorporated business but the benefits to which the directors are entitled may be higher. Provided adequate contributions have been paid, directors are normally entitled to receive unemployment and other benefits, although the Department of Trade and Industry Redundancy Payments Service will seek to restrict claims of controlling directors upon the insolvency of the company.

Employees are able to 'contract out' of the State Earnings Related Pension Scheme (SERPS) by taking out a personal pension plan.

1.3.5 Directors' liability

Principally the directors of a limited company are not exposed to the same financial risk as the sole trader or partner. If they are shareholders, their financial liability in normal circumstances is restricted to the nominal value of their shareholding unless, in the case of a public company, the number of shareholders falls below two for a period of more than six months. In these circumstances, the sole shareholder can then be jointly and severally liable with the company for payment of the company's debts contracted after that period. If directors hold no shares, they have no financial exposure.

There is, however, a contingent liability, whether or not directors hold shares, but it only arises if the directors either go beyond the limits of the authority given to them by the company's memorandum and articles of association or act recklessly or fraudulently. If they act honestly and reasonably, ultimate responsibility rests with the company and claims can only be made against company assets.

1.3.6 Administration and records

Certain records and financial information must be filed with the Registrar of Companies and so can be obtained from Companies House by the general public. Some documents must also be available for public inspection at the company's registered office and business premises on payment of a nominal fee, so that outsiders can assess the company's financial standing.

1.3.7 Accounts and reports

Accounting records must comply with the Companies Act and annual accounts must be filed with the Registrar, together with the directors' and the auditors' reports, unless only abbreviated accounts are filed or the company is exempt from the requirement to have an audit. The increase in costs should be counterbalanced by the benefit of professional monitoring of the company's activities and performance. Compliance costs can be significantly higher for public companies, which have heavier duties under company legislation and, as listed companies, must also comply with the Listing Rules of the Financial Services Authority, Alternative Investment Market (AIM), Ofex and other applicable listing regulations. A director's responsibilities as regards the annual accounts are discussed in more detail in **Chapter 4**.

1.4 The company's constitution

The memorandum of association and articles of association deal with the company's organisation, administration and the rights and obligations of the shareholders.

1.4.1 The memorandum of association

The memorandum is the company's charter and sets out its basic constitution and its powers and duties as a legal person. There are standard forms of memorandum of association prescribed by legislation for both public and private companies. These can, however, be tailored to fit individual cases.

The memorandum must be signed by at least one subscriber for a private company and two for a public company – it is they who put up the initial issued capital. The clauses of the memorandum must state:

(a) *The company's name*, the last word of which, unless it is registered (or re-registered) with unlimited liablity, must be 'limited'. The addition for a public company is 'public limited company', or 'plc', and Welsh equivalents can be used for companies whose registered office is in Wales.

(b) *The country in which its registered office is to be situated.* Normally this is in England, Scotland or Wales to establish domicile, which, unless management and control are elsewhere, means the company pays U.K. tax and operates under either English or Scottish law.

(c) *The objects for which the company is formed.* That is, a definition of the area of business activities to be undertaken – to make a profit is implied, but every other object must be set out, including the directors' investment and borrowing powers.

The principal objects are usually supplemented by other very widely drawn clauses, so that almost any ancillary activity which might be regarded as benefiting the company is covered. It is best to include several possibilities, stating that any of them can be the main and independent object of the company, so that the search for profits can be flexible.

The Companies Act 1989 provides that a company's power to enter into a transaction cannot be called into question by reason of anything in its memorandum of association. Therefore, anyone dealing with the company in good faith is entitled to assume that the directors' powers to bind the company are unrestricted. Should a particular transaction be outside the company's powers, then the directors can be held personally liable for any loss suffered by the company irrespective of any subsequent ratification by shareholders. In order to avoid any problem, objects clauses should be widely framed and ought to include the clause permitted under the 1989 Act, whereby the company is stated to be a general commercial company carrying out any trade or business whatsoever, having all the relevant powers to do so.

(d) *The liability of the members*, stating that it is limited.

(e) *The amount of initial nominal (or authorised) capital* and how it is divided into shares. The percentage subscribed for either in cash or in exchange for assets is the issued share capital; any balance remaining is unissued capital. If the company goes into liquidation, the shareholders' liability is limited to the nominal value of the shares held. The capital clause can also deal with shareholders' class rights, but they are more often set out in the articles. Any reference to share capital on the company's business stationery must quote the issued capital, not the nominal figure.

(f) *The names of the subscribers (signatories) to the memorandum* – there must be at least one for a private company and two for a public company – stating that they want to be formed into a company and that they agree to take out at least one share each.

1.4.2 The articles of association

The articles deal with internal organisation, the company's relationship with the shareholders and the relationship of the shareholders with each other, the issue of share capital, the appointment and internal powers of directors, and proceedings at meetings. Standard articles of association are set out in the company legislation, but you will usually want to make changes, which again should only be made after you have taken specialist advice.

1.4.3 Single member companies

The shares in private companies can now be held only by a single member, whereas the previous requirement was to have at least two members.

1.4.4 Electronic communication

In December 2000, the Companies Act 1985 (Electronic Communications) Order 2000 (SI 2000/3373) introduced changes to the law so that businesses and individuals are now able to file specified documents at Companies House electronically without 'live' signatures on them, in such form and manner as directed by the Registrar.

1.5 Limited Liability Partnerships (LLP)

For the sake of completeness, mention must be made of LLPs, a new form of body corporate introduced by the Limited Liability Partnerships Act 2000 which came into effect on 6 April 2001. Although the pressure on Government to introduce LLPs came primarily from large professional practices seeking to cap the personal liability of their partners, most of the LLPs registered in the first year have been for small trading businesses.

As a body corporate, the LLP is granted a certificate of incorporation, and hence has its own legal personality separate from its members (i.e., the partners). The basic process of registering an LLP is very similar to that of a limited company. It has to lodge an incorporation document with the Registrar of Companies, but an LLP does not have a formal constitution, or the equivalent of a company's memorandum and articles of association. Whilst all partnerships are well advised to have a formal written partnership agreement, this is not a public document.

1.5.1 Liabilities of the members

Where a partnership registers as an LLP, the principal advantages from the partners' viewpoint, when compared to an unlimited partnership, are that as individual members they:

- no longer have joint and several personal liability for the actions of other members;
- have no personal liability for the debts and liabilities of the LLP, as the LLP is a body corporate;
- will not be personally liable to contribute to the assets of the LLP, except to the extent provided by statute. However, it is probable that a member who is personally involved in a transaction and gives negligent advice, will be personally liable to the client for that negligent advice – particularly if they are professionally qualified.
- will not personally be liable for liabilities of the LLP incurred before the partner became a member.

1.5.2 General

Other points of interest:

(a) for taxation purposes, an LLP is treated as a partnership;
(b) subject to the rules of any relevant professional association, an LLP can issue debentures and create charges over its assets to secure any partnership borrowing;
(c) the members of the LLP are the owners of the business and hence there is no distinction between 'directors' and 'shareholders'.

1.5.3 The downside of incorporation

As a quid pro/quo for limited liability, an LLP has many of the same obligations of a private limited company to disclose information to the public about itself as set out in the LLP Regulations 2001. It must also comply with certain provisions of the Companies Act including the need to:

- maintain proper, accounting records;
- file audited accounts annually at Companies House, prepared in accordance with the provisions of the Companies Act;

- comply with the rules relating to accounting reference dates;
- file an annual return at Companies House;

Although an LLP is a corporate body, it does not have the ability to issue shares to third parties to raise equity capital;

Should an LLP become insolvent, the insolvency procedures in the Insolvency Act 1986 relating to companies apply, and the members of the partnership are potentially liable to compensate creditors for any wrong doing in the same way as company directors. Thus, the responsibilities and liabilities of the members of an LLP with regard to their creditors are very similar to those of the directors of a private limited company.

As a word of caution, it is essential that anyone contemplating either creating an LLP to conduct their business, or converting from a general partnership to an LLP, obtains specialist professional advice. There are taxation, legal, cashflow and other business implications which will need to be assessed but these will be individual to each particular partnership.

2 Directors and their responsibilities

Private companies must have at least one director and public companies at least two, and the articles may prescribe the maximum number of directors. The company must also have a company secretary who cannot be the sole director.

2.1 Who is a director?

Anyone, whatever his title and however appointed, who acts as a director will be regarded as a director: for instance councillors or committee members who run their organisation. (See De facto directors, in **2.3**.)

2.1.1 Who can be a director?

Anyone can be appointed as director unless disqualified by the articles except for:

(a) an undischarged bankrupt, unless the appointment is approved by the court;
(b) someone disqualified by court order;
(c) the company's auditor;
(d) anyone over 70, unless permitted to act by the articles or, in a public company, where the appointment is approved by the shareholders in general meeting.

The articles usually disqualify anyone of unsound mind or who is absent from board meetings for more than six months without consent. A company can be a director of another company and directors need not hold shares, unless required to do so by the articles.

2.1.2 Appointment of directors

The first director(s) is appointed by the subscribers to the memorandum, who must sign and lodge with the Registrar the formal statement of first Directors and Secretary, together with details of the company's Registered office.

Subsequent and additional appointments of directors are made in accordance with the provisions of the articles, which may provide for appointment by specified shareholders in proportion to their holdings. The usual provision, however, permits appointment by the board to fill casual vacancies or to appoint additional directors, subject to a specified maximum. Unless the articles provide otherwise, the new director must then retire at the annual general meeting following appointment and immediately stand for election by the shareholders. The shareholders must have 28 days' notice of the proposal.

The company must file a notice of appointment of each director with Companies House. The director must sign this to indicate consent to act. The appointment is effective even if a notice of appointment is not filed.

Directors are required to notify their usual residential address to the Registrar of Companies for the public record unless they have been granted a 'confidentiality order' for reasons of personal security. Beneficiaries of a confidentiality order must provide the Registrar with a service address, which will be clearly denoted as such on the public record, and their usual residential address for the confidential record access to which is restricted to 'Competent Authorities' only.

2.1.3 Retirement and removal

Very often a third of the directors are required to retire by rotation each year, standing for reappointment at the annual general meeting, unless the articles otherwise provide, and are technically out of office until reappointed by the shareholders.

In the case of listed companies, the code of best practice as set out in the Combined Code, recommends that all directors should be required to submit themselves for re-election at regular intervals, and at least every three years.

Removal is by the shareholders' simple majority vote, but 28 days' special notice of the proposal must be given to the company. The company must then immediately advise the director concerned, and give not less than 21 days' notice of the meeting to the shareholders.

2.1.4 The board of directors

The directors cannot act alone but must work collectively through the board which – whether or not it holds formal meetings, and these are often dispensed with in the small family-controlled company – usually conducts and controls company business. The board can, however, delegate its powers to one or more board members and appoint a managing director.

2.2 Directors and meetings

2.2.1 The annual general meeting

The company must hold an 'annual general meeting' within 18 months of incorporation and once in every subsequent calendar year at, at most, 15-month intervals.

If appropriate, the annual general meeting:

(a) receives the accounts and the directors' and, unless exempt from the requirement for an audit, the auditors' reports;
(b) elects the directors;
(c) if required, appoints or reappoints the auditors and fixes their remuneration;
(d) approves dividends – the directors can only make recommendations as to dividend in their report;
(e) any other 'special business'.

However, a private company may, by elective resolution, dispense with the holding of the annual general meeting, the laying of accounts, and with the reappointment of the auditors.

2.2.2 Other general meetings

All other company business, for instance alteration of the memorandum and articles or a change of name, is special and requires an 'extraordinary general meeting' with notice to shareholders and the auditors in accordance with the articles. The meetings can be called by the directors or, subject to the articles, a minority of the shareholders; in exceptional circumstances a single shareholder can ask the Secretary of State to order a meeting. The chairman or managing director of the board usually runs these meetings, although the shareholders can elect anyone to do so unless the articles prevent it.

Shareholders in a public company can assign their vote to a proxy to attend and vote at meetings on their behalf. In a private company where the rules can be more flexible, in that the proxy also has the same right as the member to speak at the meeting, notice of the meeting can be waived, or shareholders can agree not to meet at all. Where it is agreed that a meeting will not be held, it is only possible to pass written resolutions by circulation to the members, if the resolution is approved unanimously. The real business of the company, however, is decided at board meetings.

2.2.3 Notification of meetings

The Companies Act lays down the notice periods required to be given to members when calling general meetings – this period excludes the day of posting and the day of the meeting itself.

Notices of company meetings can be sent electronically to those entitled to receive them either:

(a) to an electronic address supplied for the purpose by the recipient; or
(b) published on a web site, in which case the recipient is to be notified of their availability on the site in a manner agreed with that recipient.

Any notice published on a web site, must be published for the period prescribed under the Companies Act. Furthermore, the notification to the recipient that the notice is available on a web site must contain certain details of the meeting. For the sake of consistency, the Companies Act has also been amended to enable proxies to be appointed electronically.

2.2.4 Board meetings

All the directors, whatever their function or title, have the same duties and responsibilities. Part-time and non-executive directors should therefore ensure they are kept fully informed of company affairs. Small companies often dispense with formal board meetings, but it is a dangerous practice. It is true that many decisions must be made on a day-to-day basis, but time-wasting argument after the event can be avoided if regular meetings are held at which the company's medium- and longer-term strategy and objectives are considered, and the decisions reached are then formally recorded.

Any director can call a meeting and notice must be given to all the directors, unless waived by consent. A company's articles may provide that notice of a board meeting need not be given to those directors resident outside the UK, although in a world of increasing globalisation and electronic communication, these provisions are now almost certainly outmoded.

2.2.5 Minutes of meetings

Minutes of the proceedings of all general shareholders' meetings must be entered into the company's minute book, together with a record of any written resolution, when agreed, as if it had been approved at a general meeting. These minutes must be available at the company's registered office for inspection by any shareholder, who is also entitled to a copy upon payment of the appropriate fee.

The company's articles normally require that proceedings at board meetings must be formally minuted and be entered in the company's statutory books. The minutes should also include a note of those directors present. They need not be a blow-by-blow account of the discussion, but should record major decisions in relation to the directors' conduct of the company's affairs. An accurate record is particularly important when contentious issues are being discussed, in case there is a need to refer back at a later date should things go wrong.

2.3 Part-time directors

In addition to full-time executive directors, the company may have:

Non-executive directors Part-time directors, usually with a specific expertise: financial, legal or technical. Since they are not involved in day-to-day management, they can make a valuable and objective contribution to board meetings. If they are properly to fulfil the purpose of their appointment, however, they should be ready, and be encouraged, to question the recommendations of the executive directors, so that proposed courses of action are properly justified and thought through. A non-executive director will not be excused from exercising the appropriate degree of skill and care because it is a part-time appointment.

Alternate directors Appointed by board members to act and speak on their behalf, normally during temporary periods of absence, provided there is a suitable provision in the articles.

Nominee directors Appointed to represent the interest of substantial shareholders. Such appointment does not permit them only to act in the interests of their principal; their duty, as with any other director, is to act in the interests of the company as a whole.

De facto directors A person who assumes to act as a director; any person who claims to act, or purports to act as a director, or who occupies the position of a director, whether or not properly appointed, may be treated as if he were a director.

Shadow directors Although not formally appointed as directors, these are persons in accordance with whose instructions the directors are accustomed to act. They may be individuals or companies (for example, the parent company) and again have the same duties and obligations as any other director. However, persons giving advice in a professional capacity will not be regarded as shadow directors.

There is often confusion as to whether a particular person is a '*de facto*' or a '*shadow*' director, in the belief that their roles overlap. In the court's view, rather than overlapping, they are alternatives and in most cases are probably mutually exclusive. The perception by third parties dealing with the company is totally different.

A '*de facto*' director, even though not properly appointed, is held out as a director by the company, and undertakes functions in relation to the company which could properly be discharged only by a director. Such an individual may well use the title of director, be involved in making the major decisions concerning the company's affairs and therefore be part of the corporate governing structure. By way of contrast, a '*shadow*' director will not claim to act as a director and will not be held out by the company as having authority to act on its behalf. The person concerned frequently operates in a hidden capacity, but nonetheless will be regarded as directing and controlling the activities of the company through the properly appointed board. The shadow director has become more familiar in recent years, as more people have sought to act as advisers or consultants to companies consequent upon their own disqualification or bankruptcy.

The purpose of the legislation is to identify those with real influence in the corporate affairs of the company. It is not necessary that such influence be exercised solely by direction or instruction – general advice, when taken together with any direction or instruction given, may well represent guidance to the board in accordance with which the directors were accustomed to act. But the directions or instructions need not extend over the whole of the company's corporate activities, nor need there be any degree of compulsion associated with them. In summary, it is sufficient for the 'shadow director' to be concerned at the most senior level and with most of those aspects of the direction of the company's affairs which are within the province of the directors.

2.4 Directors as employees

Directors are employees of the company and full-time executive directors should be employed under a service contract which sets out the terms and conditions of employment including pension arrangements, the level of contributions to be paid for life assurance, and details of benefits in kind. It is advisable to take legal advice before contracts are signed, as directors have no rights under the articles to remuneration, notice or compensation for loss of office, though they can claim under employment legislation. Contracts which exceed five years but cannot be terminated by the company by notice must be approved by the company in general meeting otherwise they can be set aside by the company.

For publicly quoted companies, the Cadbury Committee recommended that approval should be given for all contracts over three years, whilst the Hampel report on Corporate Governance, published in January 1998, wanted all directors' contract periods to be reduced to a maximum of one year, as soon as practicable.

Directors' service contracts must be available for inspection by members at the company's registered office or principal place of business, and if there is no written contract, there must be a written memorandum or note of the terms of employment. Details of the place of inspection, if not the company's registered office, must be sent to the Registrar.

Directors can normally claim compensation for early termination of their service contract, assuming they have one. In the absence of a contract, directors, as employees, can claim compensation for loss of office under the employment legislation, as well as for redundancy payments.

However, when the Department of Trade and Industry Redundancy Payments Service is required to make payments of this nature, normally upon the formal insolvency of the company, they will only do so currently when satisfied that the director is a genuine employee, rather than a 'controlling' shareholder director.

A director will be regarded as having a 'controlling' interest where he:

(a) effectively controls a majority of the issued shares; or
(b) is not subject to any control or guidance; or
(c) does not have a contract of service or employment; or
(d) waives salary for more than six months.

Thus any principal director of a family company may not be regarded as an employee by the Department of Trade and Industry Redundancy Payments Service and hence will not be entitled to receive any payments under the Employment Rights Act 1996. Even the waiving of salary for more than six months to assist the company's cash flow may prejudice the director's status.

2.5 Directors' duties

Directors must comply with the Companies Act and the general law and they have three primary duties:

(a) a fiduciary duty to the company to act honestly and in good faith and in the best interests of the company as a whole;
(b) a duty to exercise such a degree of skill and care, when carrying out their duties as a director, as might reasonably be expected from someone of their ability and experience;
(c) a duty to carry out the statutory obligations imposed by the Companies Act and other legislation.

2.5.1 Directors and the company

The director is a constitutional monarch bound by the terms of the company's charter, set out in the memorandum and articles, and can exercise all the powers permitted by them that are not reserved to be exercised by the shareholders in general meeting. Nevertheless, the exercise of these powers must be solely for the purposes for which they were granted.

If the director is the majority shareholder and sole director, the rule may be despotic but must remain within the specified limits. For instance, raising company loans without the power to do so can result in the director being personally responsible to both the lender and the company, if the shareholders refuse to ratify the transaction in a general meeting.

2.6 Fiduciary duty

The duty to act honestly and in good faith and in the best interests of the company imposes a trustee's responsibility on the directors to take proper care of the assets and ensure that payments are properly made and supported by adequate documentation. Directors must not make a personal profit at the company's expense. If they have an interest in transactions in which the company is involved, the nature of their interest must be disclosed to the other directors at a meeting of the board, even if disclosure appears merely to be a formality. In small companies it is also a wise precaution to make a formal minuted disclosure to shareholders.

Directors must not put themselves in a position where personal interests conflict with those of the company and must not use company property, including knowledge acquired through the company, for personal benefit. This would include, for example, the use of company assets, or the exploitation of its patents for their own use, or procuring the sale of company assets to a company controlled by themselves, or perhaps even recommending the payment of dividends, which would be advantageous to themselves as substantial shareholders but might be to the detriment of the company – where funds should be retained for future business development. These restrictions would not apply to the owner of the unincorporated business.

2.6.1 Directors as agents

Essentially a director acts as agent for the company, acting on the principal's (the company's) instructions, express or implied; so that if, for example, the director enters into a contract on behalf of the company, this binds the company. However, any action taken in the director's own name or the mere omission of the word 'limited' in documentation may result in a personal liability falling on the director.

2.6.2 Business contracts

The directors must disclose to the rest of the Board any personal interest, and the interests of any persons connected to them, whether direct or indirect, in a contract or proposed contract with the company.

This disclosure must be to the first Board meeting which considers the transaction and unless the articles specifically allow him to do so, the director must thereafter take no further part in any discussion or voting. If the interested director votes at the meeting, when the articles do not authorise him to do so, the transaction can be set aside. In certain circumstances details of the transaction must also be shown in the audited accounts.

2.6.3 Substantial property transactions

Directors and connected persons cannot acquire from or sell to the company non-cash assets worth more than £100,000 or 10 per cent of the company's net assets – provided that is more than £2,000 – without the shareholders' consent. Without such consent, the company can have the transaction set aside and reclaim the asset or claim compensation from the director for any loss suffered, or require an account of any profit.

'Connected persons' are defined as the director's spouse, children and stepchildren under 18, a trustee of a trust under which the director (or connected person) is a beneficiary, the partner of a director or connected person and an associated company. An associated company is one in which the director has either one-fifth voting control or holds at least one-fifth of the nominal equity shares.

2.6.4 Loans, credit arrangements and guarantees

A company, public or private, cannot make loans to directors or to the directors of its holding company, or provide guarantees or securities in connection with loans, unless the loan is less than £5,000, the loan or credit arrangement is part of an intergroup transaction or the credit is under £10,000. The company can, however, advance funds to directors to a maximum of £20,000 to enable them to meet properly incurred business expenses.

A public company or member of a group which includes a public company cannot extend credit to directors or connected persons, unless the company makes loans within the ordinary course of its business.

2.6.5 Share dealings

There is no restriction on directors' shares and debenture dealings, as long as the company is kept informed and details are entered on the company's register, except in the case of public companies, where restrictions are aimed at preventing directors from obtaining a personal profit from access to insider information.

Dealings in the shares of companies which are traded on the public exchanges, such as the Stock Exchange, Alternative Investment Market, Ofex, or EASDAQ must comply not only with the Companies Act, but also with the specific controlling legislation and the regulations of the various markets.

2.6.6 Insider dealings

The insider dealing provisions of the Criminal Justice Act 1993 forbid any manipulation of price-sensitive information, which has not been made public, for personal advantage. A director who knowingly, or who could reasonably be expected to have known, deals in the shares of the company or advises someone else to deal in them on the basis of confidential price-sensitive information is guilty of a criminal offence, and may be liable to account to the company for any gains made. A director must not trade in an option to buy or sell a specified number of shares at a fixed price within a specified time.

Inside knowledge can represent information obtained by directors not just about their own company, but about any others with which they come into contact. Under the Act insider dealing will be punishable by an unlimited fine and/or imprisonment for up to seven years. Insider dealing is also covered by the City Code on Takeovers and Mergers (the Code) and the Model Code for Securities Transactions by directors of listed companies.

2.6.7 Political donations and expenditure

Shareholder approval is required for any donations to political parties, and for expenditure made on behalf of political parties or EU political organisations, where in aggregate these exceed £5,000 in a year. For these purposes 'expenditure' is considered to include the cost of any additional paid leave granted to employees who serve either as MPs, local councillors or trade union officials and are therefore allowed additional paid holiday to pursue these activities.

Political donations must be approved by shareholders; the directors will be required to repay with interest, any amounts not properly authorised.

2.7 Skill and care

A person who accepts the office of director of a company undertakes the responsibility of ensuring that he understands the nature of the duty a director is called upon to perform. That duty will inevitably vary according to the size and business of the company and the experience or skills that the director holds himself out to have in support of his appointment to the office. Professionally qualified directors should therefore act with the care and diligence expected from a member of their profession. Unless directors act in a part-time or non-executive capacity, they should devote themselves full-time to their job. Although non-executive directors are required only to attend board meetings regularly, they must exercise an independent standard of judgement, and not be mere figureheads 'rubber stamping' the decisions of the full-time directors.

There is, however, no objective standard and the degree of skill and care depends on the facts and the circumstances of the individual, the job, and of that person's own knowledge and experience. Nevertheless, all directors must recognise that they have, both collectively and individually, a continuing duty to acquire and maintain a sufficient knowledge and understanding of the company's business to enable them to properly discharge their duties as directors.

Thus a director who is not an expert, may, in appropriate circumstances, rely upon suitably qualified specialists, but if he becomes aware that something is wrong, then he would be at fault if he did not attempt to put matters right.

In *D'Jan of London Ltd*, Lord Justice Hoffman stated that when determining whether a director has exercised 'due skill and care' in the course of his normal duties, the benchmark for the duty of care owed by a director is accurately described in the Insolvency Act in relation to wrongful trading. It is the conduct of:

> 'a reasonably diligent person having both:-
> (a) the general knowledge, skill and experience that may reasonably be expected of a person carrying out the same functions as are carried out by that director in relation to the company; and
> (b) the general knowledge, skill and experience that director has.'

Since that judgement, these benchmarks, one objective and the other subjective, have been widely accepted as representing those by which individual directors should be judged when determining whether they have properly exercised 'due skill and care' in the performance of their duties. In the court's view, the office of director has certain minimum responsibilities and functions. These cannot be discharged properly by leaving everything to the other directors, as the function of 'directing' requires some consideration of the company's affairs to be exercised by the person appointed. The basic standard of general knowledge, skill and care expected of any director, is that which can reasonably be expected of a reasonably diligent person who has taken on the office of director. The standard required is not lowered simply because a director either takes no active part in the company's management or has other roles within the company.

Since 1986, the Courts have played a key role in raising the basic threshold of the standard of skill and care expected of directors through a series of cases brought under ss6 and 7 of the Company Directors Disqualification Act. One such case, *Barings plc (No 5); directors and rogue traders*, which is discussed in more detail in **Chapter 8**, is now widely regarded as a 'land mark' case in this area of the law. The judge considered the previous legal authorities on the content of directors duties, from which he derived three general propositions, the first of which was:

> 'Directors have, both collectively and individually, a continuing duty to acquire and maintain a sufficient knowledge and understanding of the company's business to enable them properly to discharge their duties as directors.'

This implies that all directors who accept office are under a positive and continuing obligation to participate in the company's affairs in some degree. The extent of the obligation will depend on a number of factors, which could include:

- the size of the company;
- the management structure;
- the role in the management of the company assumed by the director and the duties expected of a person in that role; and
- the experience and skills of the particular director.

Nevertheless, there is a minimum requirement that a director informs himself sufficiently about the company's business to enable him to perform his functions.

Therefore, anyone becoming a director for the first time, should appreciate that claiming ignorance of a director's duties and responsibilities because one is 'new to the job' will not be an acceptable defence if things go wrong.

2.7.1 Delegation

In all but the smallest of companies, some degree of delegation is probably essential if the company's business is to be carried on efficiently. Subject to the articles of association of the company, a board of directors may delegate specific tasks and functions, but when duties are delegated, directors, like any other employer or contractor, must be satisfied that they are delegating to a suitable person who is honest, competent and reliable.

In the absence of any grounds for suspicion, directors are entitled to trust their employees' competence and integrity to a reasonable extent. However, delegation does not absolve a director from the duty to question whether the management system in place is operating efficiently and whether individuals, to whom duties have been delegated in accordance with the system, are discharging those duties diligently.

The second general proposition put forward by Judge Parker in the Barings plc (No 5) case as mentioned in the previous section enforced this view:

> 'Whilst directors are entitled (subject to the articles of association of the company) to delegate particular functions to those below them in the management chain, and to trust their competence and integrity to a reasonable extent, the exercise of the power of delegation does not absolve a director from the duty to supervise the discharge of delegated functions.'

In the course of this case he concluded that the whole board and each director 'remain responsible for the delegated function or functions and will retain a residual duty of supervision and control'.

Thus overall responsibility is not delegable – and the higher the office within an organisation that is held by an individual, the greater the responsibilities that fall upon that person.

2.8 Statutory duties

2.8.1 Administrative duties

Administrative obligations are mainly contained in the Companies Acts 1985 and 1989 and the Insolvency Act 1986. The Companies Act 1989 introduced new measures, mostly by way of amendment to the 1985 Act, to implement the provisions of the European Union's Seventh and Eighth Company Law Directives on group accounts and the regulation of auditors. Certain company law requirements have also been amended.

Failure to comply with the requirements – and there are some 200 statutory offences – may result in fines and/or imprisonment or disqualification. Both the company and its officers can be liable for fines, either imposed as a lump sum or accruing on a daily basis. Persistent, albeit technical, default can lead to the directors being disqualified from acting as a director or from being involved, directly or indirectly, in company management for up to 15 years. Accordingly directors, particularly of smaller companies, often pass these duties to their accountants or solicitors, who are experienced in dealing with company administration, leaving them free to concentrate on day-to-day management. This is appropriate delegation of duty, but the directors still retain their own duty to supervise and they remain ultimately responsible for ensuring that the company complies with legal requirements.

A company must now comply with a wide range of legislation, many examples of which are included in **Table 2**. If it fails to do so, the directors may become personally liable for any penalties imposed under the law or for any loss suffered by a third party.

Table 2: **Relevant legislation includes:**
Employees
Access to Medical Reports Act 1988
Asylum & Immigration Act 1996
Companies Act 1985
Data Protection Act 1998
Disability Discrimination Act 1995
Disabled Persons (Employment) Acts 1944 & 1958
Employment Acts 1980 & 1990
Employment Relations Act 1999
Employment Rights Act 1996
Equal Pay Act 1970
Factories Act 1961
The Health and Safety (Consultation with Employees) Regulations 1996
Management of Health and Safety at Work Regulations 1992
National Minimum Wage Act 1998
Part-time Workers Regulations 2000

Pensions Act 1995
Protection from Harassment Act 1997
Protection of Children Act 1999
Public Interest Disclosure Act 1998
Race Relations Act 1976
Road Traffic Acts 1960 to 1982
Sex Discrimination Act 1975
Trade Union Act 1984
Trade Union and Labour Relations (Consolidation) Act 1992
Transfer of Undertakings (Protection of Employment) Regulations 1981
Wages Act 1986
Welfare Reform and Pensions Act 1999
Working Time Regulations 1998

Premises
Clean Air Act 1993
Control of Pollution Act 1974
Employer's Liability (Compulsory Insurance) Act 1949
Employer's Liability (Defective Equipment) Act 1969
Environmental Protection Act 1990
Environment Act 1995
Factories Act 1961
Health and Safety at Work etc. Act 1974
Occupiers' Liability Acts 1957 and 1984
Offices Shops and Railway Premises Act 1963
Water Resources Act 1991

Revenue
Value Added Tax Act 1983
Income and Corporation Taxes Act 1988
Taxes Management Act 1970
Betting and Gaming Act 1972

2.8.2 Statutory books

The statutory requirements relating to the maintenance of company records are technical and it is therefore usually cost-effective, particularly for a smaller company, for professional advisers to maintain them and to file the necessary documentation.

A limited company, unlike a sole trader or partnership, is required to maintain certain registers, providing details of shareholders, directors and other related matters. Details from these records must be filed at Companies House and the books must be available for public inspection during business hours at the company's registered office or principal place of business, on payment of a nominal fee. The registers are a useful record of the company's business activities and participants and comprise:

(a) the register of members;
(b) the register of debenture holders;
(c) the register of directors and secretaries;

(d) the register of directors' interests in the company's shares;
(e) the register of charges;
(f) minutes of the shareholders' meetings (available to members only).

Usually the company secretary maintains the statutory books but in many smaller companies they are kept by the company's accountants. Access is normally free to members but a small charge is made to others.

Changes to the entries in the registers must be filed with the Registrar, as must any change in the company's registered office, copies of all special and extraordinary shareholders' resolutions, together with any changes in the memorandum and articles and certain ordinary resolutions. The Registrar must also be notified of a change in the company's accounting reference date (that is, its financial year end), and must receive an original signed copy of the financial statements, or for a small or medium-sized company (see **4.1**) a signed copy of its abbreviated accounts. Details of share issues as well as the annual return must also be filed with the Registrar.

2.8.3 The annual return

This basically summarises the information contained in the statutory books and some of the changes during the year. Returns also have to provide details of the company's principal business activities.

Every company has a 'return date' which for new companies is the anniversary of the date of incorporation and for existing companies is the anniversary of the date of the last return. The annual return has to be made up to date not later than its return date, and then filed with the Registrar of Companies within 28 days of its completion.

Companies House operates a 'shuttle' document service whereby it sends a draft annual return to the company for amendment, as necessary, which can then be returned with the annual filing fee. Failure to submit a return or to maintain the records and supply the information renders the directors and officers liable to a fine. Persistent failure to comply with the requirements may lead to disqualification of the directors and to the company being struck off by the Registrar.

2.9 Duties towards employees

The obligations imposed by the legislation relating to employees and business premises, which bring liability for third-party claims affected by the company's business activities, apply to all employers. The directors are, of course, responsible for ensuring the company complies with the law but because of the protection afforded by limited liability, claims are usually made against the company. Nevertheless, in some circumstances, for instance where there is fraud or negligence, the company can turn to the individual concerned, director or employee, for a contribution or indemnity.

Since 1990 there has been a dramatic expansion of employment legislation and case law, much of which has been derived from European directives and cases heard in the European Court. Following their election in 1997, the commitment of the Labour Government to accept the Social Chapter was widely expected to lead to many new laws emanating from the European Union which impose ever-increasing obligations upon both companies and their directors. As **Table 2** shows, this forecast has proved to be only too accurate.

Therefore, it is essential that directors take advice from appropriately qualified professionals to ensure that their own company procedures are adequate to protect both the company and the directors. It is important to realise that employment law generally, and in particular that relating to discrimination and pensions, has become exceedingly complex. Specialist advice is necessary to confirm that the relevant regulations have been complied with by the company, and hence, directors avoid the possibility of their unknowingly running the risk of prosecution.

2.9.1 Discrimination

In the past claims for wrongful and unfair dismissal or for discrimination on the grounds of either race, sex or disability were usually brought against the employer on the basis that the organisation had the funds to pay any compensation awarded. Although a director cannot be held personally liable for an unfair dismissal, directors can find themselves personally liable for a claim for wrongful dismissal (i.e., breach of a contract of employment) if it is shown that they were responsible for inducing the company to commit the breach of contract.

Similarly, in claims against employers for discrimination, if the company can show that it has taken 'such steps as are reasonably practicable' to inform employees about its equal opportunities and anti-discrimination policies, the company may well be absolved from liability. For this reason, those responsible for directing these policies within the company may be cited as respondents in any action alleging discrimination and this is not uncommon in practice. Therefore, those directors who have direct or indirect responsibility for staff training, disciplinary procedures, promotion or provision of benefits should be aware that they can bear individual liability if any of their acts or omissions are deemed to have caused an act of discrimination.

The establishment of effective procedures within the company to deal with these issues is even more important now that there is no ceiling on the monetary compensation that can be awarded by the court for successful discrimination claims.

2.9.2 Employee rights

As indicated earlier, a significant part of the 'employee' legislation enacted since 1997 reflects those European directives intended, either directly or indirectly, to protect the rights of employees. It is clearly impossible in a book of this nature, to provide a comprehensive review of this body of law, but only to highlight the more obvious recent statutes, which include:

- the Regulations relating to the Transfer of Undertakings now require employers to consult with their employees, or the employees' elected representatives, prior to any relevant business transfer, or where there are going to be more than 20 redundancies at any one establishment;
- Public Interest Disclosure Act 1998 – (the Whistleblower's Act) – makes the victimisation of employees for disclosure of unethical practices unlawful;
- Data Protection Act 1998 – employee personal data needs to be kept securely and can only be used for proper purposes. Employees have the right of access to this information.

Regulations relating to the rights of posted and part-time workers, working times, fixed team workers and parental leave are also being introduced; a breach of these regulations may result in criminal charges being brought against the employer.

This is yet another area upon which directors may now need to take specialist advice to ensure the regulations, when finalised, are complied with.

2.9.3 Health and Safety

The Health and Safety at Work, etc. Act 1974 imposes a general duty on all employers to take appropriate steps to ensure the health and safety of their staff and to reduce the risk to others affected by work activities. More detailed regulations concerning the requirements of the Act were introduced in 1999 – these include the need for employers to:

- appoint a competent person to be responsible for health and safety matters;
- provide employees with information about the risks they face and the company's protective measures to control those risks;
- consult employees as appropriate on health and safety issues;

As with environmental offences, where a company commits a health and safety offence with the consent or connivance of a director, or is the result of his negligence, then a claim may be brought against that director personally.

2.9.4 Occupational pension schemes

The Pensions Act 1995, 187 pages in all, enacted a formidable tranche of legislation, which including the associated sets of regulations, runs to over two million words. The Act is wide-ranging and will have an impact on many occupational pension schemes. The Occupational Pensions Regulatory Authority (OPRA) is the statutory organisation created by the Pensions Act to be responsible for the regulation of occupational pensions, and has the power to impose civil penalties and to prosecute both individual trustees and companies. Therefore, both the employer and trustee risk incurring penalties if the statutory requirements are not met and, for the trustees, the ultimate penalty could be imprisonment.

The impact on sponsoring employers

The Minimum Funding Requirement (MFR), which applies to salary related (defined benefit) schemes, was introduced by the Pensions Act 1995 (PAQS) to help make occupation pensions more secure. Where a scheme has a deficit, the sponsoring employer has to agree a schedule of contributions to make good that funding deficit within a specified period of time.

For many employers this has led to the need to make higher regular contributions or one off special lump sum payments. Unfortunately, a scheme which is apparently fully funded does not necessarily ensure that all of the scheme's liabilities can be met should the scheme be wound up. Clearly, actuarial advice is essential.

Under Financial Reporting Standard (FRS)17 'Retirement Benefits' a defined benefit pension scheme surplus or deficiency, is due to be shown on the balance sheet of the sponsoring employer for accounting periods ending on or after 22 June 2003. However, it is now understood this will be deferred by two years.

The future of the MFR is limited, as on 7 March 2001 the Chancellor of the Exchequer announced the Government's intention to abolish it at some time. It is likely to be replaced with a long term scheme specific standard, in conjuction with other measures to protect scheme member's interests.

Sponsoring employers are now required to pay the employees' contributions to the scheme's trustees within 19 days of the end of the month in which they were deducted from their employees' pay. The employer's contributions must also be paid to the trustee by the due date agreed – the making of payments on account during the year, with a top-up after the year-end is no longer acceptable. Under the Act, failure to pay employee contributions to the trustees on time is a criminal offence and the employer may be fined, imprisoned or both. OPRA also have the power to impose penalties in respect of late payment of employee contributions.

2.10 Environmental responsibilities

The increasing awareness of the consequences of the damage that our industrialised society is inflicting upon the environment has resulted in the passage of a mass of 'green' legislation since 1990, with the major statutes being the Environmental Protection Act 1990 (EPA 1990) and the Water Resources Act 1991 (WRA 1991), as supplemented by the Environment Act 1995. In addition, there is a substantial body of regulations, guidance notes and codes of practice. One result of the legislation is that individuals involved in the management of companies causing pollution may be personally liable for environmental offences.

Criminal liability is a common feature of the environmental legislation, and so not only can companies or other forms of business organisation, be prosecuted for breaches of the law, but so can directors or managers responsible for running those organisations. All the major environmental statutes contain provisions which specify that directors, officers and senior employees may be found liable for environmental offences. For example, s157(1) EPA 1990 provides that:

> 'Where an offence under any provision of this Act committed by a body corporate is proved to have been committed with the consent or connivance of, or to have been attributable to any neglect on the part of, any director, manager, secretary or other similar officer of the body corporate or a person who was purporting to act in any such capacity, he as well as the body corporate shall be guilty of that offence and shall be liable to be proceeded against and punished accordingly.'

'Consent' to an offence implies the positive agreement to a particular act by a director, whereas 'connivance' can have a much wider meaning, and can include situations of which the director was either aware or ought to have been aware, but simply failed to take any action to prevent it.

Table 3: Major environmental legislation and regulatory authority in England and Wales

Area	*Legislation*	*Authority*
Integrated pollution prevention and control	Pollution Prevention and Control (England and Wales) Regulations 2000 (Part A(1) installation and mobile plants)	Environment Agency
Local authority integrated pollution prevention and control and air pollution control	Pollution Prevention and Control (England and Wales) Regulations 2000 (Part A(2) and Part B installations and mobile plants); Clean Air Act 1993	Environment Health Departments of Local Authorities
Water pollution	WRA 1991; Anti-Pollution Works Regulations 1999	Environment Agency
Waste	Pt II EPA 1990	Environment Agency
Registration of waste carriers	Control of Pollution (Amendment) Act 1989	Environment Agency
Packaging waste	Producer Responsibility Obligations (Packaging Waste) Regulations 1997	Environment Agency
Statutory nuisances	Pt III EPA 1990	Environmental Health Departments of Local Authorities
Trade effluent into sewerage systems	Water Industry Act 1991	Water and sewerage undertakers
Planning	Town and Country Planning Act 1990; Planning (Hazardous Substances) Act 1990	Planning Departments of Local Authorities

The EPA establishes offences relating to the unlawful deposit of waste and the WRA 1991 establishes offences for the pollution of rivers, streams, lakes, groundwater and coastal waters. Depending on the statute, the Crown Court can impose either unlimited fines or imprisonment for up to five years, with magistrates courts having authority to impose lesser sanctions.

In addition to environmental offences, legislative provisions authorise regulatory authorities to serve remediation notices requiring persons who cause or knowingly permit the presence of pollution and, in some instances, owners or occupiers of contaminated land, to remediate the pollution. Other provisions authorise the Environment Agency to serve works notices on persons who cause or knowingly permit pollutants to enter surface waters, groundwater and coastal waters. Yet other provisions authorise the Environment Agency to order the operator of an installation, such as a commercial or industrial facility, to suspend operations if these involve an imminent risk of serious pollution.

The responsibility for enforcing environmental legislation is mainly vested in the Environment Agency (for England and Wales), the Scottish Environment Protection Agency and local authorities. A summary of the major environmental legislative provisions and the regulatory authorities which enforce them is contained in **Table 3**.

In November 1998, the Environment Agency issued its enforcement and prosecution policy in respect of directors and officers, which provides that:

> 'Criminal proceedings will be taken against those persons responsible for the offence. Where a company is involved, it will be usual practice to prosecute the company where the offence resulted from the company's activities. However, the Agency will also consider any part played in the offence by the officers of the company, including directors, managers and the Company Secretary. Action may also be taken against such officers (as well as the company) where it can be shown that the offence was committed with their consent, was due to their neglect or they "turned a blind eye" to the offence, or the circumstances leading to it. In appropriate cases, the Agency will consider seeking disqualification of directors under the Companies Act'.

The following cases demonstrate that environmental issues are now regarded much more seriously than in the past and that breaches of the EPA will be pursued vigorously by the Environment Agency.

During 2000 the Agency successfully prosecuted seven directors and cautioned two others.

- In late 1997, St Albans Crown Court sentenced a director to 10 months and 18 months imprisonment for two offences concerning waste, the sentences to run concurrently. The first sentence was imposed for abandoning nine 40–foot-long trailers and three roll-on containers containing waste in an industrial facility in Hoddesdon. The second sentence was for abandoning over 100 tonnes of waste, including bags of clinical waste, bins of hypodermic needles, scalpels and other sharp instruments and medibins of body tissues and amputated limbs in a warehouse in Hertford.
- In June 1998, Bradford Crown Court sentenced the director of a defunct drum cleaning company to 60 hours community service for breaching the terms and conditions of an authorisation under the integrated pollution control regime. The breaches included exceeding emission limits for

dioxin, acid gases, volatile organic compounds, particulates and metals. The director had pleaded guilty to five of 12 specimen charges brought by the Environment Agency.

- In November 2001, the Chester Magistrates Court fined the director of a golf club £1,000 for two counts of knowingly permitting construction and other waste to be deposited at the Mollington Grange Golf Club. The waste had been used as landscaping. The director of the golf club was also a director of the company that had provided the construction waste.
- In December 2001, the West Berkshire Magistrates Court fined the managing director of Southern Refining Services £10,000 with £900 in costs for three counts of breaching the company's authorisation under the integrated pollution control regime and two counts of knowingly permitting the discharge of effluent to groundwater. The court also fined the company. The incident leading to the prosecution involved approximately 10,000 litres of effluent from a tank containing solvents being discharged through a hose to surface water drains adjacent to the facility.
- In an extreme example of pollution in the Thames Estuary, the Environment Agency prosecuted Pharmacos Limited, a company which traded as a chemical repackager, and its managing director, Mr Brown. Mr Brown had instructed his employees to use a new method to prepare mercury nitrate solution, despite warnings from two employees, both chemists, that the procedure was unsafe. There was a violent chemical reaction, which led to the release of nitrogen dioxide fumes and mercury into the estuary. Subsequently Mr Brown gave instructions for the process to be repeated and again nitrogen dioxide was released. As the company had no authority to carry out this process, the Environment Agency prosecuted; proceedings were also brought against the managing director who was both fined and disqualified from being a company director.

Thus, a basic understanding of environmental legislation and the principles behind it is needed by directors if they are to avoid personal liability. However, as this area of law is technical and complex, directors should ensure that the company's activities are regularly reviewed from an environmental perspective, with particular attention being given to those activities which might cause pollution. It may well be advisable also to check the terms of any directors' and officers' insurance policy the company has taken out, to establish whether any protection is afforded.

Directors should also consider introducing an environmental policy and, further, an environmental management system for their companies. Issues addressed in an environmental management system could include, for example, waste management, emissions to the atmosphere, contaminated land, noise, discharges to water, the storage of hazardous materials and nuisance. The European Community's Eco-Management and Audit Scheme (EMAS) and the international ISO 14001 standard are the two major standards for environmental management systems. The standards, which are voluntary, require internal auditing to check the effectiveness of, and compliance with, the objectives of a company's environmental management system. In addition, EMAS specifically requires verification by an independent third party.

At present there is no requirement in the UK for companies to disclose details of environmental matters in their annual reports, although there is a requirement under FRS 12 to report details of certain environmental liabilities in a company's financial statements. Nevertheless, some companies, mostly listed, do provide some information on these matters either in their annual reports or in separate environmental reports.

3 Directors and corporate governance

Basic governance issues concern the effectiveness and accountability of boards of directors to the company's shareholders. In the case of public companies, institutional shareholders are being encouraged to take a more active role in scrutinizing the performance of the board, and to exercise their right not to reappoint those directors who fail either to perform, or to comply with accepted best practice. There is now significant pressure upon all organisations, whether publicly owned or private, to be transparent in their dealings with those with whom they do business. However, perhaps not surprisingly, private companies remain significantly less accountable than their publicly listed counterparts.

Although the Combined Code on Corporate Governance is directed primarily at the boards of listed companies, it comprises a set of principles of good corporate governance and a code of best practice which all companies would do well to emulate.

3.1 Background

In May 1991, the Financial Reporting Council, the London Stock Exchange and the accountancy profession set up a review panel, chaired by Sir Adrian Cadbury, to report on the financial aspects of corporate governance and to consider, in particular, the responsibilities of directors in relation to accounting matters.

3.1.1 Cadbury Code

When the Cadbury Report was published in December 1992, it defined corporate governance as the system by which companies are directed and controlled and identified three key elements in the process – the Board, the shareholders and the auditors. The Board was responsible for ensuring the company complied with the 'Cadbury Code', and in their report on the annual accounts was required to report to shareholders the extent to which this had been done. The auditors provided an objective check on the directors' statements.

3.1.2 The Greenbury code

Subsequently, in 1995, a study group chaired by Sir Richard Greenbury, was set up to review the disclosure requirements for directors' remuneration for publicly listed companies. 'Greenbury' was established in the wake of the general concern about the very substantial remuneration packages awarded to some directors, particularly in the privatised utilities. As a consequence the 'Greenbury' code set out in reasonable detail the information that the committee recommended should be disclosed in the annual accounts.

3.1.3 The Hampel report

Both the Cadbury and the Greenbury codes were established as responses to areas of specific concern – irresponsible company management and excessive remuneration. The Hampel Committee was set up in November 1995 with a brief, inter alia, 'to seek to promote high standards of corporate governance' and to review the Cadbury code and any relevant matters arising from the Greenbury report. They were to consider afresh the roles of directors, shareholders and auditors in corporate governance.

When their final report was published in January 1998, for the most part Hampel endorsed the findings of the two previous committees, and did not consider any major changes were necessary. However, the committee were concerned that the emphasis on accountability within the Cadbury and Greenbury codes had tended to obscure a board's primary responsibility – namely to act in the best interests of the shareholders by enhancing the prosperity of the business over time. Nevertheless, in their view, good governance should ensure that the different stakeholders with an interest in a company's business – employees, customers, suppliers, financiers, local communities and governments – are also taken into account.

This principle is reiterated in the Company Law Review's report, which favoured the current view that directors owed their duties exclusively towards shareholders with the objective of maximising shareholder value, whilst at the same time acknowledging the requirement to properly understand, assess and manage the interests of the wider community in which the company operates.

3.2 The Combined Code

The Combined Code as it now stands is derived from the Cadbury, Greenbury and Hampel reports. Whilst it draws largely from the conclusions of the Hampel report, the Code remains consistent with the three elements of governance, which formed the basis of the Cadbury code, namely:

- the composition and role of the board of directors, including the determination of the Board's remuneration;
- the role of, and relationship with, the company's shareholders;
- the Board's relationship with the company's auditors and the function of the auditors.

Part 1 of the Code, reproduced below, sets out 17 principles of good governance, some of which are applicable to listed companies only, but compliance with the Code is mandatory for fully listed companies.

Section 1 Companies

A Directors

The Board

1 Every listed company should be headed by an effective board which should lead and control the company.

Chairman and CEO

2 There are two key tasks at the top of every public company – the running of the board and the executive responsibility for the running of the company's business. There should be a clear division of responsibilities at the head of the company which will ensure a balance of power and authority, such that no one individual has unfettered powers of decision.

Board balance

3 The board should include a balance of executive and non-executive directors (including independent non-executives) such that no individual or small group of individuals can dominate the board's decision taking.

Supply of information

4 The board should be supplied in a timely manner with information in a form and of a quality appropriate to enable it to discharge its duties.

Appointments to the board

5 There should be a formal and transparent procedure for the appointment of new directors to the board.

Re-election

6 All directors should be required to submit themselves for re-election at regular intervals and at least every three years.

B Directors' remuneration

The level and make-up of remuneration

1 Levels of remuneration should be sufficient to attract and retain the directors needed to run the company successfully, but companies should

avoid paying more than is necessary for this purpose. A proportion of executive directors' remuneration should be structured so as to link rewards to corporate and individual performance.

Procedure

2 Companies should establish a formal and transparent procedure for developing policy on executive remuneration and for fixing the remuneration packages of individual directors. No director should be involved in deciding his or her own remuneration.

Disclosure

3 The company's annual report should contain a statement of remuneration policy and details of the remuneration of each director.

C Relations with shareholders

Dialogue with institutional shareholders

1 Companies should be ready, where practicable, to enter into a dialogue with institutional shareholders based on the mutual understanding of objectives.

Constructive use of the AGM

2 Boards should use the AGM to communicate with private investors and encourage their participation.

D Accountability and audit

Financial reporting

1 The board should present a balanced and understandable assessment of the company's position and prospects.

Internal control

2 The board should maintain a sound system of internal control to safeguard shareholders' investment and the company's assets.

Audit committee and auditors

3 The board should establish formal and transparent arrangements for considering how they should apply the financial reporting and internal control principles and for maintaining an appropriate relationship with the company's auditors.

Section 2 Institutional shareholders

E Institutional investors

Shareholder voting

1 Institutional shareholders have a responsibility to make considered use of their votes.

Dialogue with companies

2 Institutional shareholders should be ready, where practicable, to enter into a dialogue with companies based on the mutual understanding of objectives.

Evaluation of governance disclosures

3 When evaluating companies' governance arrangements, particularly those relating to board structure and composition, institutional investors should give due weight to all relevant factors drawn to their attention.

3.2.1 Internal controls

The Combined Code also introduces a 'new principle' into corporate governance, which was not included in the Cadbury, Greenbury or Hampel recommendations, that requires all listed companies to maintain a sound system of internal control to safeguard the shareholders' investment in the company's assets. The detailed provisions require the directors to review, annually, the effectiveness of the group's system of internal controls including financial, operational and compliance controls and risk management. Companies should also review the need for an internal audit function.

Yet another committee – The Turnbull Working Party – was then set up to provide guidance to companies as to the steps they should take to comply with these provisions. They recommended that listed companies should have an internal control system that monitors important threats to the company, such as environmental, ethical and social risks. Although it is left to individual companies to judge for themselves what constitutes a sound system of internal control, the responsibility for internal risk management rests with the directors and the executive management. However, if weaknesses in internal control have resulted in material losses requiring disclosure in the annual accounts, then the directors must set out in the accounts details of the corrective action taken, or an explanation as to why no action is necessary.

3.2.2 Corporate governance and the 'OMB'

The remit of the Hampel committee was limited to listed companies but their report deliberately avoided distinguishing between the governance standards expected from both larger and smaller companies. In their view, any distinction by size would be arbitrary, but nevertheless it was recognised that flexibility would be required when determining the standards of corporate governance applicable to the smaller-listed company or to owner-managed businesses (OMBs).

At first sight, Sections C and E of the Code dealing primarily with the company's relationship with Institutional shareholders may be regarded as being of less relevance to OMB's. Nevertheless, there are many very useful messages in the Code for smaller, proprietor controlled companies here. For example, family businesses requiring additional capital to fund expansion or who are seeking an exit route because of lack of succession within the family, may well need the assistance of external providers of equity capital. Where a third party funder does become involved, they will almost certainly expect the company to have reasonable standards of corporate governance, appropriate to the size of the business.

In these circumstances, the appointment of an independent non-executive director with experience of governance issues can assist in the management of the relationship with the outside investor as well as helping the company put the appropriate management structure and procedures in place.

3.3 The role of the non-executive director

The Cadbury committee undoubtedly raised the profile of the non-executive director, although the importance of the non-executive's function as monitor of the executive directors was perhaps over-emphasised to the detriment of the other benefits of such appointments. Obviously the key to the success of any appointment is to choose the right person – it is essential that the 'chemistry' is right if an outsider is going to become an effective member of the team. The board as a whole must not only accept that there is a role for the non-executive director but, furthermore, all members should understand what that role should be.

One of the key tenets within the Combined Code is the importance of having independent non-executive directors on the board. When directors are all members of the same family it is very easy to dispense with formal board meetings, or for the areas of responsibility to become blurred. The presence of a part-time non-executive director may encourage a degree of formality which, in smaller companies, can make individuals consider rather more carefully the consequences of a particular decision. It is beneficial for well-established and frequently unquestioned policies to be reviewed periodically to ensure that they are still appropriate.

There are many other ways in which an experienced non-executive director can contribute to the development of a growing business, for example:

- provide specialist expertise;
- contribute to strategic development;
- provide greater knowledge of the industry;
- facilitate relationships with third parties; and
- raise the company's profile.

If the existing directors are relatively new to formal company procedures, the non-executive can also:

- improve formal board procedures;
- assist in promoting management changes;
- monitor compliance with best practice; and
- act as confidant to the chief executive.

It is frequently suggested that a strong non-executive can act as a counterbalance to a forceful managing director, but in practice this combination is simply likely to make for noisy board meetings! To be effective, any non-executive must be seen to be truly independent. He must be prepared to resign should they find themselves in serious disagreement with their colleagues over board policy.

Independence will almost certainly be compromised if a non-executive:

- is or has recently been employed by the company;
- is employed by a major customer or supplier;
- is related to other board members or senior management;
- is retained as a professional adviser, or is a partner in a firm advising the company; or
- is financially dependent upon the remuneration received.

3.3.1 Term of office

Non-executive directors should have a specific term of office in the same way as their executive colleagues, and be subject to the usual re-election process. As one of the objectives of appointing non-executives is either to bring in specialist knowledge or fresh ideas, a relatively short period of office, of say five years, may well be appropriate. Experience will vary widely, but over time, the same person may become less able to provide the fresh perspective which is frequently the great benefit of an independent appointment.

3.3.2 Prospective appointments – some questions to ask

Before gratefully accepting a company's invitation to join the board, it is essential that any prospective appointee undertakes a comprehensive 'due diligence' exercise on the company itself. This is particularly important because the potential liabilities of a non-executive director are just as onerous as those of the executive directors, but the non-executive does not have the same ability to directly manage or influence the company's performance as his executive colleagues.

Any prospective non-executive needs to be vigilant before accepting an appointment – he should do much more than simply visit the company and talk to the senior employees. Many questions need to be asked, both of the company and of the prospective appointee, which would normally include at least some of the following, particularly when considering an appointment with smaller private companies.

- What does the Company do?
- What is the board's view of the company's market place?
- What is the company's reputation in the eyes of third parties – customers, suppliers, trade associations, bankers etc.?

What are the shareholders strategic objectives?

- Where do they *want* the company to be in five years time?
- Where do they *expect* it to be in five years time?
- Are their expectations realistic?
- Are shareholder's objectives consistent with those of management?

Of the company
What is the structure of the board?

- Is it dominated by the founding entrepreneur, or by family members?
- Are there any obvious gaps in the board's skill base; if so how are these to be filled?
- Are there any other non-executive directors – if not how effective is a single non-executive likely to be?
- What is the age profile of the board and senior management; how has succession been addressed?
- How regularly does the board meet? – Ask to see recent minutes.

How is the role of the non-executive perceived?

- Why is the appointment being made?
- What contribution/expertise are the board expecting from the non-executive?
- What is the time commitment?

How reliable is the company's management information?

- Is management information produced regularly?
- How do the results of the most recent audited accounts compare with the management accounts to the same date?
- Are business plans and forecasts available for review?
- Does the company have adequate procedures and systems of internal control in place?
- What issues are raised by the auditors' in their management letters?

Of the non-executive

- Is the role clearly defined, and agreed by the Board as a whole?
- Will I be able to work with the other board members – will we get on?
- How important is industry specific knowledge?
- Will I be given sufficient information to be able to do the job properly?
- What do the board minutes tell me?
- Is the remuneration appropriate for the job – but at a level where, if necessary, I can afford to resign without difficulty.

A good non-executive needs to be able, independent of mind, but politically sensitive – in the right context, the appointment can be rewarding and very worthwhile for both the company and the individual.

4 Directors and the accounts

4.1 The annual accounts

The Companies Act requires the directors to prepare a profit and loss account for each financial year (the accounting reference period), and a balance sheet as at the same date to which the profit and loss account is drawn up. The accounts should be prepared in accordance with generally accepted accounting principles, and comply with the relevant accounting standards as laid down by the Accounting Standards Board.

For a company incorporated before the Companies Act 1989 came into force, the accounting reference date is 31 March, unless the company notifies the Registrar of an alternative date. The accounting reference date for companies incorporated since then will normally be the last day of the month in which the anniversary of incorporation falls. However, these companies can elect to change their accounting reference date, at any time before their first accounts become overdue for filing. With the exception of the first accounting period, which can be for any period up to 18 months, the accounting reference period is normally 12 months.

Unless otherwise authorised by all the shareholders the annual financial statements, including the directors' report, must be presented by the directors to the shareholders at the annual general meeting and then filed with the Registrar. Unless the company is exempt from the requirement to have an audit, the statements must have been audited and be accompanied by the auditors' report. Apart from first accounting period, when special rules apply, private companies must file accounts within 10 months of the accounting reference date but public companies must file them within 7 months. Even if a company has become dormant, that is, there have not been any transactions during the accounting period which ought to be entered in the books of account, accounts must still be filed, although, provided certain formalities are observed, they do not have to be audited.

Where the company has remained dormant since incorporation, the directors can file a Dormant Company Accounts Form at Companies House, instead of preparing and filing full financial statements.

Fines are imposed for late filing starting at £100 and £500, respectively, for private and public companies.

Small and medium-sized companies and groups are defined by the Act by reference to turnover, balance sheet totals and number of employees, as set out in **Table 4**. Fulfilment of two out of the three criteria is sufficient to categorise the company or group as small or medium-sized; where a company is likely to change it's status, special rules apply.

***Table 4*: Companies Act criteria for small and medium companies.**

	Small *£m*	*Medium* *£m*	*Small group* *£m*	*Medium group* *£m*
1. Turnover is not more than	2.8	11.2	2.8 net or 3.36 gross	11.2 net or 13.44 gross
2. Balance sheet total (i.e., total of fixed and current assets) is not more than	1.4	5.6	1.4 net or £1.68 gross	£5.6 net or £6.72 gross
3. Monthly average number of employees does not exceed	50	250	50	250

The format of the accounts is set out in the Companies Act: a small company may file with the Registrar an abbreviated balance sheet with accompanying notes and is not required to file a profit and loss account or directors' report. However the format for a medium-sized company is very similar to a full set of accounts, in that the only concession is that turnover and cost of sales need not be disclosed.

Although, at first sight, this concession appears to reduce costs, the Act does not permit any company to present abbreviated accounts to its members. Therefore, it is necessary for both small and medium-sized companies to distribute a full set of accounts to their members, although for a small company, these can be 'abridged accounts' which omit certain of the disclosures required in a full set.

A copy of the accounts must also be sent to every holder of any debentures issued by the company and to every person entitled to receive notice of general meetings, which includes the auditors. This can be done electronically, either directly to the parties, or by publication on the company's website in which case the recipients must be told of their availability there. If accounts are published on the web, the directors must acknowledge they are responsible for the controls over and the security of the website and for establishing and controlling the process for electronically distributing annual reports and other financial information to shareholders.

4.1.1 Group accounts

A parent company need not prepare group accounts either for distribution to members or for filing purposes, if the group qualifies as small or medium-sized according to **Table 4**. Companies and groups cannot take advantage of these exemptions if they (or any of their member companies) are a public company, a banking, shipping or insurance company, or an authorised person under the Financial Services and Markets Act 2000. Parent companies can only qualify as small or medium if the group they head also qualifies as a small or medium group.

However, although group accounts need not be prepared, details of the subsidiaries' results and capital and reserves do have to be presented and the directors' report must also disclose certain group information. In addition, the parent company's auditors are required to satisfy themselves that the company is entitled to exemption from preparing group accounts.

The Companies Act does grant a UK company controlling a group exemption from preparing consolidated accounts in a number of circumstances. These include:-

(i) if it is a wholly owned subsidiary of a company incorporated in Great Britain.

(ii) UK companies whose immediate parent is situated elsewhere in the European Union, are also exempt from preparing consolidated accounts provided that the immediate parent itself produces consolidated accounts which include the UK group. These accounts, which have to be filed with the Registrar of Companies, must be either in English or accompanied by a translation.

This exemption does not apply if any of the shares are listed on a Stock Exchange in any member state of the European Union.

However, a 'subsidiary' is now far more widely defined, and has regard to the parent's ability to control another undertaking, whether through voting rights, the right to appoint directors or the right to exercise a dominant influence over the subsidiary's affairs. When referring to subsidiary undertakings, the definition includes unincorporated businesses, details of which may have to be included in the group's consolidated accounts.

4.1.2 The directors' report

The Companies Act specifies what should be covered in the directors' report. Broadly it must describe the principal activities of the business, giving details of any material changes, and review developments through the year.

The report also sets out what the directors recommend should be distributed by way of dividend; there are usually significant tax and legal implications here, and professional advice is essential. In addition, details of the directors, their shareholdings and other interests in the company must be shown.

Statement of directors' responsibilities
Unless a statement of the directors' responsibilities for the preparation of the financial statements for each financial year is shown separately in the financial statements, the auditors should include such a statement in their audit report. In particular, the directors are required to:

(i) select suitable accounting policies and then apply them consistently ;
(ii) make judgements and estimates that are reasonable and prudent;
(iii) state whether applicable accounting standards have been followed, subject to any material departures disclosed and explained in the financial statements (for large companies only); and
(iv) prepare the financial statements on the going concern basis unless it is inappropriate to presume that the company will continue in business.

The directors must also acknowledge that they are responsible for ensuring that the company keeps proper accounting records which disclose with reasonable accuracy at any time the financial position of the company and to enable them to ensure that the financial statements comply with the Companies Act 1985. They also accept responsibility for safeguarding the assets of the company and hence for taking reasonable steps for the prevention and detection of fraud and other irregularities.

The Listing Rules require a statement to be included in the company's annual report and accounts setting out how the company has applied the principles of the Combined Code and whether these have been adopted throughout the accounting period. Sufficient explanation must be given in this statement to enable shareholders to evaluate how the principles of the Code have been applied.

Reasons for any non-compliance must be given. The Code also requires directors to report to shareholders whether they have conducted a review of the effectiveness of the company's system of internal controls at least annually. As noted in the previous chapter, the review should cover all controls, including financial, operational and compliance controls and risk management. Hence it has certainly proved to be one of the most onerous provisions of the Code.

The directors' report must be formally approved by the board and signed on its behalf by either a director or the company secretary. The auditors are required to be satisfied that the report is consistent with the accounts.

4.1.3 Directors' remuneration

The Directors' Remuneration Report (DRR) regulations 2002, aim to strengthen the disclosure requirements for public companies quoted on major exchanges, whether in the UK or overseas. A quoted company is likely to be required to produce a DRR in conjunction with its annual audited accounts. This report, which is likely to be required for accounting periods ending on or after 31 December 2002, will provide:

- a statement on future remuneration policy;
- a graphical comparison of the company's performance over the last five years;
- an explanation of company policy as regards the length of directors' service contracts, notice periods and termination arrangements.

It is intended to give the shareholders the right to vote to approve the DRR at the AGM, which would give shareholders more information and an opportunity to voice their opinions.

4.2 The auditors

A sole trader, partnership or company requires accounts for efficient management, to raise additional finance and for submission to the Inland Revenue when determining their tax liability. The proprietors of a company protected by limited liability must, unless exempt from the requirement to have audited accounts, also have independently audited accounts, and the auditors are required to report on the accounts to the shareholders.

At the present time a company is exempt from having an audit if it qualifies as a small company, its annual turnover is not more than £1 million and its balance sheet total does not exceed £1.4 million. There are separate rules for companies that are members of a group upon which professional advice should be sought. Shareholders owning at least 10 per cent of the issued share capital can require an audit to be carried out. As with the option to file abbreviated accounts, this exemption is not available to a public company, a member of a group, banking or insurance company, an insurance broker, an authorised person under the Financial Services and Markets Act 2000, an employer's association or a registered body under the Trade Union and Labour Relations (Consolidation) Act 1992.

The auditors must be professionally qualified and be members of the Institute of Chartered Accountants in England and Wales, the Association of Chartered Certified Accountants, or members of the Scottish or Irish Institutes of Chartered Accountants. They cannot be directors or employees of the company or the partner of a director or employee.

4.2.1 Appointing the auditors

In the first accounting period the auditors may be appointed by the directors; thereafter appointment and reappointment must be approved by the shareholders at the annual general meeting. Auditors can be removed at any time by ordinary resolution, that is, by a majority vote of the shareholders, provided they are given notice of the resolution.

4.2.2 The auditors' report

The auditors must report to shareholders on the annual accounts and their report must be attached to those accounts which are circulated to the shareholders. In their report they are required to state:

(a) that the directors are responsible for the preparation of the accounts and for the maintenance of adequate accounting records and controls;
(b) the responsibilities of the auditors and the work undertaken by them; and
(c) whether the accounts give a true and fair view of the state of the company's affairs and of its profit or loss for the period and whether they have been properly prepared in accordance with the Companies Act 1985.

The auditors also have to be satisfied that proper accounting records have been kept and that the accounts presented agree with those records.

In order that they can properly carry out the audit, the auditors must be given an unrestricted right of access at all times to the company's books, vouchers and other documentation. They can require the directors and other officers to supply as much information as they consider necessary to enable them to perform their duties. If a director, either knowingly or recklessly, misleads the auditors, then he is guilty of an offence and is liable to either imprisonment or a fine.

The auditors are also entitled to attend and, if they think it necessary, address any general meeting of the company – in addition to the annual general meeting – and neither the scope of the audit nor these statutory rights can be restricted by the directors. Accordingly, it is now common for directors to be asked formally to record that they have provided the auditors with all the information relevant to the company's financial position and required for the preparation of the accounts. The auditors have a duty to report to shareholders if they have any qualifications or reservations on the accounts or as to the information and explanations given to them by the directors.

Where companies have adopted the Combined Code recommendations, which are mandatory for listed companies, then the auditors are required to review how the company has complied with the Combined Code provisions, and have a responsibility to report any non-compliance with these to the shareholders if this is not disclosed elsewhere in the accounts.

4.3 Accounting records

All businesses should maintain detailed and up-to-date accounting records. Many business failures might have been avoided if accurate financial information had been readily available. In order to protect third parties, the Companies Act requires a limited company to maintain proper accounting records which must include:

(a) entries of all cash receipts and payments on a daily basis, including details of the transactions to which they relate and a record of the company's assets and liabilities;
(b) if the company deals in goods (as opposed to services) a statement of stock held at the end of each financial year, together with details of stock takings on which the records are based;
(c) with the exception of the retail trade, a sufficient description of goods bought and sold to enable the sellers and purchases to be identified.

The accounting records must also disclose, with reasonable accuracy, the financial position of the company at any one time.

Records must be held either at the registered office or at such other place as agreed by the directors and be available for inspection by the company's officers. The directors of all companies preparing group accounts are required to ensure that the accounting records of any subsidiary undertaking, whether an unincorporated business or a limited company, are adequate to enable proper accounts to be prepared. If adequate records are not maintained, the directors and other officers in default may be fined and/or imprisoned.

4.3.1 Management accounts

Any company, large or small, should maintain its accounting records in such a way that management accounts can be prepared quickly and cost effectively on a monthly or quarterly basis. Good management accounts prepared from accurate accounting records may also help to reduce the cost of preparing the annual financial statements and of the annual audit.

For the smaller company, it may be cost effective to turn to the company's external accountants for assistance, rather than employ a full-time finance director or chief accountant. With their specialised knowledge the accountants can advise on the form and content of these accounts to ensure they provide the key information required to control effectively the day-to-day operation of the company.

To make profits the directors have to take the right decisions. To do this they need the right information, in the right format at the right time. Regular management accounts need not be complicated, but they should cover:

Profitability	Relevant information here would include information on sales, the gross margin earned (possibly differentiating by product if appropriate), overheads and other expenses. It is often sufficient simply to use monthly gross margin and overheads figures based on annual budgets, although the actual labour costs should usually be available and therefore incorporated in the figures.
Cash management	Levels of stock, debtors and creditors should be monitored and future capital expenditure requirements taken into consideration, so that cash resources are properly controlled.
Budgets and forecasts	Effective control is not based solely on historical information; future prospects should be assessed and annual budgets prepared, which should incorporate cash flow projections. The actual results achieved should then be compared regularly with the budget and the results for the previous year. Any significant variances should be investigated, so that corrective action can be taken where necessary.

Here again, the external accountants or auditors can be of real assistance and the documentation can form the basis for a properly prepared approach to the company's bankers, whose response to a request for an extension of credit facilities is likely to be far more positive if supported by up-to-date, professionally prepared documentation.

The statutory requirements for proper accounting records are only a minimum in the context of a fully effective management accounting system. In the larger and more complex business, much more detailed and sophisticated accounting records may be necessary to maintain financial and management control.

By far the most common cause of company failure is inadequate or sometimes non-existent accounting records. The legislation puts responsibility squarely on the directors to ensure that these records are adequate and maintained on a regular basis. Trading while insolvent brings personal liability and if the directors cannot ascertain the company's true financial position, they may unwittingly incur personal liability for any debts the company cannot pay. Under the provisions of the Company Directors Disqualification Act 1986, they may also face disqualification if the court has concluded that there has been either fraudulent or wrongful trading.

If the directors regularly review the management accounts with their external accountants any potential problem this reveals can be discussed, so that action can be taken promptly before major difficulties arise.

5 The Company Law Review ('CLR')

5.1 Overall objectives

A Steering Group to undertake the review was established in early 1998 by the Secretary of State at the Department of Trade and Industry with a brief to report within three years. The Review Group summarised their terms of reference broadly as follows:

> 'To make recommendations that would create 'a framework of company law' which:
> - promotes the competitiveness of British companies;
> - strikes a proper balance between the interests of the various groups concerned with company activity within an appropriate framework of regulation; and
> - promotes consistency, predictability and transparency of the law.'

It has been widely accepted for some years that current legislation governing the formation, operation and dissolution of companies requires reform. The majority of British company law is contained in the Companies Act 1985 which is derived from nineteenth century legislation, updated and added to intermittently as the need arose. The Companies Act and a host of other statutes are supplemented by a substantial body of case law which enshrines fundamental principles of major areas of law – for example, the duties of directors to their company. As a result, current legislation is unduly complex and detailed, difficult to understand, and in part outdated.

Therefore the Review Group sought to establish a coherent body of law from the patchwork of piecemeal legislation, but to do this, they considered they needed to:

- establish a coherent definition of the responsibilities of directors, shareholders and auditors;

- establish a proper relationship between company law and non-statutory standards of behaviour as prescribed in the codes of Corporate Governance;
- encourage more transparency in the affairs of larger companies;
- assess the use of new technology to communicate information.

It is outside the scope of this book to cover fully the recommendations of the Review Group – the reader is referred to their final report published in July 2001 and to other texts listed in the bibliography for more information in that regard. However, it is important that their recommendations in relation to the duties and conduct of directors are appreciated by anyone who is either a director currently, or is contemplating becoming one. It must be emphasised that the proposals outlined in this chapter may differ from the eventual legislation approved by Parliament. Nevertheless, given the extensive consultation process undertaken between 1998 and 2001, the fundamental thrust for greater simplicity is unlikely to alter.

5.2 The role of a director

The Review Group considered the role of the director to be at the heart of company law; they are the individuals who direct a company's operations, its relationship with third parties and its impact on the local community and environment. In the Review Group's opinion, the law governing the activities of directors has two purposes:

- to regulate the private relationships between the directors, their company and the company's shareholders; and
- to serve the wider public interest.

However, the Review Group concluded 'that it would be impractical to create duties for directors that were owed to and enforceable by a wider constituency than the shareholders, and hence rejected the view that directors' duties should be owed to a wide number of disparate parties. In their opinion, a director's duty should remain exclusively due to the shareholders, but capable of being enforced on their behalf by the company. Nevertheless, it was accepted that directors should be required to properly understand, assess and manage the wider interests of their employees, suppliers, customers and the local community in which they operate.

The Review Group agreed that there is a need to codify directors' general duties, and recommends that there should be an exhaustive legislative restatement of directors' duties to their company, expressed at a high level of generality. The intention should be to provide clear, accessible and authoritative guidance for directors, which can be consistently applied by the courts.

Although significant, the reforms proposed do not radically alter or replace the responsibilities of directors currently found in the legislation or in case law as discussed in the rest of this book. For the most part they seek to codify and simplify the law, so that in future, company directors should find it easier to understand.

5.2.1 Directors' duties – general principles

The Review Group's final report includes a draft statement of directors' duties – it also recommends that a schedule of general principles by which directors are bound should be incorporated into the legislation. The general principles are intended to replace the existing equitable and common law rules, and impose upon directors obligations owed to the company, but these obligations would remain subordinate to those imposed by statute.

The general principles represent a codification of the duties embodied in case law currently, and hence the precedents established by the courts are relevant.

A summary of the general principles is set out below.

Obeying the constitution
To obey the company's constitution and decisions taken either under the constitution or the general law; directors to use their powers only for their proper purpose.

Promotion of company's objectives
Directors owe a duty of loyalty to their company – to act in good faith in a way most likely to promote the success of the company for the benefit of its members as a whole. When doing so, a director must take account of all the material factors it is practical to identify.

Delegation and independence of judgement
A director should exercise independent judgement when exercising his powers, and not delegate these except in accordance with the constitution of the company.

Care, skill and diligence
To exercise care, skill, and diligence in accordance with the test established by the courts in accordance with s214 IA. This involves both subjective and objective standards that would be exercised by a reasonably diligent person with:

- the knowledge, skill and experience reasonably expected of a person in the director's position;
- the general knowledge, skill and experience which the director has.

As a consequence a director can be personally liable should he fail to exercise the care and skill which would reasonably be expected of a person in his position in the company having regard to his qualifications and experience.

Conflict of interest
A director has a duty to disclose to the company any personal interest in any transaction entered into by the company. This would represent a relaxation of the present rule whereby directors are required to account to the company for any personal benefit arising from a transaction entered into by the company in which he has an interest.

Personal use of company property
A director should be prohibited from using company property or knowledge for his own benefit, without the approval of either the shareholders, or of the board of directors (excluding the interested director). At present, authorisation can only be given by the shareholders or by the company's constitution.

Benefits from third parties
Benefits received by directors in connection with the exercise of their duties are only acceptable if their receipt is either approved by ordinary resolution of the shareholders, or if the benefits are necessarily incidental to the proper performance of the director's functions.

Special duty prior to possible insolvency
At a time when the directors ought to recognise that the company at some point in the future is more likely than not, to be unable to pay its debts as they fall due, the duty to promote the company's objectives may cease to be paramount.

The greater the risk of insolvency, the more the directors should have regard to the interests of the creditors, in priority to those of the members.

Special duty where no reasonable prospect of avoiding insolvent liquidation
In these circumstances the director's prime duty is to exercise due skill and care in taking every step to minimise the potential loss to creditors.

5.2.2 Directors as employees

Service contracts
In the interests of greater transparency, full details of all directors' service contracts and any ancillary arrangements for both executive and non-executive directors should be disclosed to shareholders. Any service contract should be made available to shareholders on request.

Service contracts should normally be for a maximum of one year, with the exception of the initial contract, which may be for a three-year term. Shareholders, by general resolution, may be able to extend these contracts but if they do, this must be disclosed in the company's annual financial statements.

Payments to directors

The Review Group proposes a number of detailed changes to the law relating to payments to directors, for example:

- repealing the prohibition on tax free payments and on directors dealing in share options;
- simplifying the law dealing with payments to directors and former directors for compensation for loss of office; payments made in accordance with an approved contact of employment should be exempt.

It is recommended that the detailed rules on disclosure should be set by a newly appointed Standards Board.

Substantial property transactions

It is intended that the present restrictions need not apply to payments made under properly approved service contracts.

Loans and credit transactions

Those restrictions, which only apply to public companies at present, should apply to all companies in future.

Business contracts

The Review Group recommends that the disclosure of a director's interest in a company contract should be restricted to a 'material' interest only, where the onus is on the director involved to determine what is material.

Sanctions against directors

Criminal offences by directors should be split into three categories:

- offences of dishonesty;
- intermediate offences;
- regulatory offences.

Only the proposed 'intermediate offence' constitutes an additional control over directors' duties, but its definition seems, at best, to be imprecise. An intermediate offence will represent an act or omission of company management, where dishonesty is difficult to establish, but strong suspicions arise. It is suggested that two distinct offences should be created to permit penalties of varying severity to be imposed:

- a failure to comply with relevant requirements; and
- to do so with dishonest intent.

New offences would include, inter alia:

- the failure, whether inadvertent or not, to disclose a director's interest in contracts with the company. If introduced, it will be particularly important for the directors of small companies to segregate their own interest from those of the company;
- the deliberate and dishonest failure to maintain proper accounting records;
- dishonestly making a false statement to the auditors, or failing to inform them of material facts.

Power of the court to grant relief
The Review Group propose that when seeking relief from the court, the onus should not be on the director to show that he has acted reasonably, but the court should be allowed to grant relief to the directors where it is satisfied that the director has acted honestly and hence ought fairly to be excused.

5.3 Company administration and governance

Many of the other recommendations of the Review Group are technical in nature, aimed primarily at simplifying the procedures associated with the formation and administration of limited companies, particularly smaller companies. If the proposals are enacted on the basis of the Review Group report, the principal areas of company law affected will be as follows.

5.3.1 Shareholders and company formation

The changes proposed are mostly either procedural or technical, and hence are not considered in detail here. In the context of a director's role, the proposals most likely to have a direct impact are:

- shareholders are to be provided with more biographical information about directors seeking election;
- the law on general meetings should be simplified;
- obligations imposed by the company's constitution will be enforceable by individual members;
- the procedure to ratify directors' wrongful acts should be simplified; however any relief given should exclude any breach of duty in relation to creditors;
- to codify into company law the existing common law rules on company distributions.

The procedure for company formation is to be updated; all companies will have unlimited capacity within a single constitution document which will replace the present Memorandum and Articles of Association.

5.3.2 Company accounts

The most significant recommendation is that companies of any size (provisionally defined in the Government's White Paper) – whether public or private – will have to include an Operating and Financial Review (OFR) as part of their annual financial statements. The OFR is to represent a general review by the directors of the company's business, its performance and future prospects and should include comment upon:

- the company's business objectives and general strategy;
- market changes, new products and services;
- corporate governance policy;
- key relationships with customers, suppliers and other third parties;
- the company's policies on environmental, community, and social issues.

In effect this is intended to replace the current Directors' Report which will no longer be necessary.

The exemptions granted for accounting and reporting purposes should remain based on size and be increased to any two of:

(a) turnover up to £4.8m (currently £2.8m);
(b) balance sheet total below £2.4m, (currently £1.4m);
(c) up to 50 employees (unchanged).

There are a number of other minor changes to the present procedures proposed which are designed to improve the quality, timeliness and accessibility of company year-end reporting. These include:

- the concept of medium sized companies should be abolished;
- the period for filing accounts should be reduced by three months for both public and private companies to four and seven months respectively;
- the accounts shall be distributed by the later of the date of filing or 14 days before the company's Annual General Meeting.

5.3.3 The auditors

The auditors are to review the process of compiling the annual OFR, and to report on the cash flow statement included in the annual financial statements.

It is proposed firstly to extend the directors' current obligation to provide the auditors with such information and explanations as they request. Secondly it is proposed to impose upon directors a requirement that they must volunteer such relevant information as would be expected to be provided by any director exercising due skill and care.

Perhaps more controversially, it is also recommended that auditors should be able to limit their liability in accordance with guidelines as yet to be determined.

5.4 The Government's response

In July 2002, the Government published a White Paper – 'Modernising Company Law' – as the first stage in the consultation process regarding the implementation of the Review Group's recommendations, of which they are broadly supportive. The minister has reiterated that the starting point for company law should be small companies – additional or different provisions should be brought in for large companies as considered necessary. The law also needs to be flexible so that it can adapt easily to ongoing development and changing technology.

5.4.1 Directors' duties

The Government agrees with the Review Group's recommendations that:

- The primary role of directors should be to promote the success of the company for the benefit of its shareholders as a whole; and
- The directors' general duties to the company should be codified broadly along the lines proposed by the Review Group, as set out in paragraph 5.2.1.

The codified statement of general duties will replace the principles established by the exisiting body of common law and a director's obligation under the Companies Act to have regard to the interests of employees. Therefore all directors of a company will be subject to the same set of general duties, regardless of any particular duties they might have under service agreements as employees. The detailed provisions are to be contained in Schedule 2 to a new Companies Bill, but on the basis of the draft clauses in the White Paper, the only significant changes from the Review Group's summary of general principles are:

a) Directors, when promoting the success of the company for the benefit of shareholders, must consider both the short and the long term consequences of their actions, to the extent that a person exercising reasonable care and skill would consider them to be relevant. The material factors to be considered are the need to:-

i. foster business relationships, including those with employees, suppliers and customers;
ii. have regard to the impact of its operations on the local community and on the environment;
iii. maintain a reputation for high standards of business; and
iv. achieve outcomes that are fair between its members.

Hopefully these objectives are not mutually exclusive, and no doubt in time, there will be further guidance given, ultimately by the Courts, as to the weight or priority that should be given to each particular objective.

b) where the director has a personal interest in any transaction which he has not disclosed, then he must not enter into that transaction with the company at all;
c) personal use of company property by a director can only be authorised by the board of a plc if the company's constitution enables the board to do so;
d) the government was not prepared to support the Review Group's recommendations that a director's duties to creditors, at a time when a company's solvency was in doubt, should also be codified. If this was done, there is concern that directors might 'run for cover' at the first sign of a company's financial difficulty by initiating formal insolvency proceedings; it was also believed that this situation was already adequately provided for by the provisions of the Insolvency Act.

5.4.2 Corporate directors

It is proposed to prohibit the appointment of any new corporate directors and after a suitable transitional period, prohibit all corporate directorships.

5.4.3 Improving governance: shareholders and decision making

The government 's stated objective is to enable small companies, in particular, to take decisions quickly and effectively. The principal proposals in the White Paper are:

Memorandum and articles of association
In future, companies are to have a constitution in a single document that will replace the present Memorandum and Articles of Association. New model constitutions in simple and clear language will be prepared by the government for both private and public companies.

The Company Law Review ('CLR')

Annual general meetings

Private companies will not have to hold annual general meetings at which they are required to present the annual accounts and reappoint the auditors, unless either:-

- the shareholders resolve to do so by ordinary resolution; or
- a single member or the auditor requisitions the company to do so.

However, the Government believes there are disadvantages in allowing single members to requisition the holding of an AGM and are canvassing views on this clause. If an AGM is to be held, this must be done within 10 months of the financial year end.

Public companies will be required to hold an AGM within 6 months of the year end, unless the members resolve unanimously that no meeting is required.

Resolutions

There will only be ordinary or special resolutions at shareholders' meetings; the latter will require 14 days notice, instead of 21 days at present.

To reduce the necessity of holding formal shareholders' meetings, private companies will be permitted to pass written ordinary resolutions by simple majority and written special resolutions, by a 75% majority. It is proposed that the electronic communication of resolutions can only be used where the resolution can be received either in legible form or in a form agreed between the member and the company which can be converted into legible form.

Company formation

The Review Group submitted a number of other technical amendments intended to simplify and streamline company administration upon which further consultation is planned. Despite doubts expressed by a significant number of respondents to the Review Group's recommendation that private companies no longer need appoint a company secretary, although the option to do so remains if they wish, it is intended to implement this proposal. In the Government's view, the role of company secretary is not essential to good governance – that is the responsibility of the directors.

Company accounts and reporting requirements

Given that around 95% of the UK companies have fewer than 50 employees, the Government agrees that the reporting requirements for small private companies should be simpler than for large private and public companies. Therefore it is proposed that the definition of a small company should be increased to the European Union Maximum set out in paragraph 5.3.2 as recommended by the Review Group. A summary of the proposals in the White Paper on reporting and accounts, is set out in Table 4A.

***Table 4A:* Summary of proposals on reporting and accounting regime**

	Small private	*Other private*	*Unquoted*	*Quoted public*
Financial statements	Yes – but no cash flow statement and simpler form and content	Yes	Yes	Yes (but form and content governed by IAS)
OFR	No *	If economically significant	If economically significant	If economically significant
Supplementary Statement	Yes – but reduced level of requirements	Yes for items not in OFR	Yes for items not in OFR	Yes for items not in OFR
Director's Remuneration Report	No	No	No	Yes
Summary statement	Optional	Optional	Optional	Optional
Date for distribution of annual reporting documents to shareholders	7 months	7 months	6 months (but effectively reduced by notice period for AGM)	6 months (but effectively reduced by notice period for AGM and requirement to publish on a website)
Date for filing annual reporting documents with registrar	7 months	7 months	6 months	6 months
Date of holding AGM (if applicable)	10 months	10 months	6 months	6 months

* Economically significant is defined as follows:

	Public	Private
Turnover exceeds	£50m	£500m
Balance sheet totals exceed	£25m	£250m
No of employees exceed	500	5000

The Company Law Review ('CLR')

Annual financial statements
In future it is proposed that the responsibility for determining the form and content of financial statements should be devolved to a new Standards Board, thereby avoiding the need for legislation when relatively minor changes are required.

It is proposed to abolish the concept of abbreviated accounts, so that all companies will have to file their full statutory accounts but small companies will not have to provide consolidated financial statements or a cashflow statement. Given that cash is the life blood of every business, the proposal that small companies need not produce a cash flow statement seems surprising, and regrettable. The great majority of companies that fail are small ones, whose management all too often did not understand properly their company's cash needs. The requirement to produce a cash flow statement might assist in some small way, in improving this very common management failing.

Auditors
The Review Group's proposals are generally endorsed, but the issue of auditor liability has not yet been addressed. The recommendation that the turnover threshold below which companies do not have to have an audit be raised from £1 million to £4.8 million has not yet been accepted, although this will be kept under review

5.5 Conclusion

Even if only a reasonable proportion of the Review Group's proposals become law, the office of director will undoubtedly become more risky. This emphasises the importance of educating prospective directors about their potential responsibilities before they assume office. The courts have made it very clear that directors are expected to understand what their duties are – for example, in *Re Austinsuite Furniture Limited*, the judge disqualified a newly appointed director because he regarded him as having been irresponsible in accepting the appointment without having any commercial experience.

Whilst the proposed schedule of general principles for director's conduct is derived from the existing body of case law, they are not intended to provide specific guidance as to how directors should act in any particular situation. Therefore directors should still obtain professional advice regarding any circumstances about which they are uncertain or which cause them concern.

6 Directors' liabilities

6.1 Civil claims

The potential liabilities of directors are very great and may even lead to their losing everything they have, but the company's liability is only passed to directors and management in specified circumstances. Personal liability, both civil and criminal, can flow from breach of statutory or other duty, or where there is fraud. A director may also be liable for the company's negligence, for example, where there is a claim for personal injury under the general law brought by an employee or outsider injured on the premises and the director is clearly at fault and in dereliction of duty.

Directors may be personally liable if they or the company, to their knowledge, act outside the powers given to them by the memorandum and articles, and if they contract without reference to the company by, for instance, placing orders without stating that they are acting on the company's behalf. The company can avoid the transaction, leaving the director personally to deal with the financial consequences. Directors can also be personally liable if they sign cheques and other negotiable instruments which do not carry the company's proper registered name.

Directors are liable for misfeasance, that is, wrongdoing – for instance, making secret profits at the company's expense. Nonfeasance, that is, doing nothing, may bring dismissal but the director is not necessarily liable for the financial consequences, unless the court regards the inaction as constituting an abdication of the director's responsibilities amounting to negligence. Under the Companies Act a director can apply to the court for relief in any proceedings for negligence, default, breach of duty or breach of trust by a director.

Thus directors will generally only become personally liable if they fail to exercise the skill and expertise that may reasonably be expected of someone in their position when acting with reasonable diligence. Thus a certain minimum standard is expected from every director, and the relevant specialist skills are required to be exercised by those fulfilling specialist roles, for example finance or technical directors. Under company law, the court may relieve a director of liability from any action for negligence or breach of duty if it is satisfied that the director acted reasonably and honestly and in the circumstances ought fairly to be excused.

6.1.1 The company and the director

Court action to recover compensation from a director can usually only be brought by the company. If it is solvent and management holds the majority of the shares and ratifies a questionable or voidable transaction, an action might be brought by a minority of aggrieved shareholders – a shareholding of one is sufficient if the complainant can show there has been unfair prejudice against the minority, or even against the interests of the members generally. The aggrieved party can petition the court to make an order giving such relief as it considers appropriate, although it may be reluctant to become involved in disputes which relate purely to the internal management of a company's affairs.

If the director has not acted in the best interests of the company as a whole, he can be ordered to compensate it for its loss, returning wrongfully acquired assets or accounting to the company for gains derived from use of its assets or knowledge acquired through the company. This would include profits from insider dealing. If there is unfair prejudice, the court can exercise strict control over the company by, for instance, ordering majority shareholders to buy out the complainant or requiring alteration of the memorandum and articles.

The court may, however, decide it is 'just and equitable' to order the company to be wound up, but the order is made only if the shareholders have no other remedy and they are not being unreasonable in insisting on a winding up. The court may authorise a small minority of shareholders to bring an action against management for the benefit of the company, for example, if the other majority shareholders do not share the profit fairly or there is other wrongdoing. However, if the board is simply inefficient, a shareholder may be able to do nothing. Run-of-the-mill negligence is insufficient, even if it leads to loss; usually there must be some manipulation of the advantage of a majority holding by which the director gained something to which he was not otherwise entitled.

As a last resort the company (by special resolution) or at least 200 or ten per cent of the shareholders can call in the Department of Trade and Industry to investigate the company's affairs, but they must have substantial grounds and must give security for the costs of the inquiry, to a current maximum of £5,000.

6.1.2 Directors and shareholders

Directors do not normally have a duty to individual shareholders, but there is an overriding duty not to deceive shareholders. The Theft Act 1968 makes it an offence for an officer of a company to publish a written statement or account of the company's affairs with the intention of deceiving the members, knowing it to be false or misleading. Also under the Companies Act directors can be held jointly and severally liable with the company to compensate any person who suffers loss if they knowingly permit the contravention of any pre-emption rights of the existing shareholders as regards new share issues.

6.1.3 Directors and groups of companies

The director of any company, whether independent or a member of a group, assumes all the associated responsibilities and potential liabilities irrespective of the level of authority granted to that person. It is essential, therefore, that the boards of companies in groups have a clear understanding of the extent of their own board's authority, for they assume all the legal and statutory obligations for those companies to which they have been appointed.

For example, if an instruction is issued by the chairman of the parent company which is deemed to be in the interests of the group as a whole, the directors of each subsidiary should consider the implications of this for their own company. Hopefully, collective action by members of the group will be beneficial for each member but there are many instances when a profitable subsidiary has been forced into insolvency because its cash resources have been drained by less successful companies elsewhere in the group. Sometimes centralised banking arrangements are set up to enable the group's overall borrowing requirements to be minimised or more frequently, cross guarantees are required by the group's bankers from all companies.

Directors must consider whether, as far as their own company is concerned , the commercial justification for entering into arrangements of this nature is reasonable and, if necessary, take independent advice as regards their duty to their own company and to its creditors. This may be particularly relevant when called upon to give guarantees in respect of liabilities of other group companies whose activities are quite unrelated.

On the other side of the coin, where a subsidiary company is effectively completely subservient to the board of the parent company, the parent company may be regarded as a shadow director of the subsidiary. In these circumstances, it does not necessarily follow that the parent company's own directors will also be regarded as shadow directors personally as long as they act only in their capacity as directors of the parent when advising or attending board meetings of the subsidiary.

Therefore, within a group, the responsibilities of individual company boards and board members need to be adequately defined, and the directors of each company should ensure that they have executive authority over their own company's affairs which is consistent with their own responsibilities.

6.1.4 Takeovers and mergers

The rights of shareholders of all companies are protected on takeovers or mergers by the Companies Act 1985. Further, for all public companies, and for private companies whose shares have either been listed or traded in the last 10 years, The City Code on Takeovers and Mergers, the Listing Rules of the FSA, and the rules governing the acquisition of shares will apply. The Code has no legal force, but is supervised by the Panel on Takeovers and Mergers which represents the collective opinion of those professionally involved in takeovers as to what constitutes proper business standards.

It relies for its effectiveness upon its power to impose sanctions within the securities market upon those who fail to observe the Code including companies, directors or individuals and their professional advisers.

6.1.5 Share issues

Company law has long sought to protect potential purchasers of company shares. Directors, amongst others, can be personally liable to compensate anyone who suffers loss as a result of subscribing for shares on the basis of a prospectus document which contains an untrue statement. For listed companies, the Listing Rules of the FSA set out the information to be contained in documents or circulars to be issued by the company to shareholders, and drafts have to be approved by the Stock Exchange before general circulation. In the case of companies wishing to trade on either the AIM or Ofex markets, the draft documents will similarly have to be approved by a duly authorised adviser.

The provisions of the Financial Services and Markets Act 2000 govern the regulation of investment business, which includes the making of any offer to the general public for the issue or sale of shares in either private or public limited companies. Such business can only be conducted by persons specifically authorised to do so under the Act. However, when shares are offered for sale, the directors of the company concerned will be held responsible for the accuracy of the information relating to the company contained in any prospectus issued or in any financial promotion document. Even when acting on the company's behalf, directors can be held personally liable under this

Act – it is certainly an offence to induce people to invest by making any statement or forecast which is known to be false or deceptive. Therefore, the directors of any company seeking to raise finance from outside sources, whether from an issue of shares to the public, from Enterprise Investment Scheme investors, or from a private placing should ensure that they are aware of the main details of this relatively complex piece of legislation.

6.1.6 Directors and taxation

All businesses are obliged to account to the Crown for tax deducted or collected from transactions made in the normal course of trading, for example, pay as you earn (PAYE) deductions made from employees' pay or value added tax (VAT) included on sales invoices. However, if the relevant tax is not accounted for, and the Crown departments believe this was the result of either dishonesty or wilful default, they are empowered to seek recompense from the employees concerned, usually a director.

In the case of VAT, as a general rule the person who signs a VAT return is responsible for the accuracy of that return, and may be liable to imprisonment for fraudulently making a false return. HM Customs & Excise can assess a penalty on a company for dishonestly attempting to evade payment of VAT, but if it appears that the dishonesty is in whole or in part, attributable to the conduct of a director, then they can assess the penalty on the director as well as on the company. There is, however, no general power available to HM Customs & Excise to ask a director to meet the company's VAT liability.

Similarly under the PAYE regulations, if it can be shown that the company had wilfully failed to make the PAYE deductions correctly and the employee received the emoluments knowing the PAYE had not been correctly deducted then the Inland Revenue can recover the PAYE from the employee. In practice the regulations are normally only operated against directors, typically after a liquidation when the company has failed whilst owing PAYE on directors' remuneration. Therefore directors should always take care to preserve copies of the relevant PAYE records, in case it becomes necessary subsequently to prove that deductions were made, and paid over.

In the case of unpaid National Insurance contributions powers were given to the Department of Social Security under the Social Security Act 1998 to enable these to be recovered from a director or other officers, where a company has failed to pay National Insurance contributions at, or within the prescribed time. If it appears to the Secretary of State that the failure is due to the 'fraud or neglect' of 'a culpable officer', the Contributions Agency can pursue both the officer and the company for the outstanding sum, plus interest. If there is more than one culpable officer, the liability is apportioned between them.

These provisions were enacted because of the government's concern about 'the phoenix company syndrome', whereby the directors of an insolvent company emerge running a new company but with virtually the same business, after their predecessor company had failed owing substantial unpaid National Insurance contributions. As this represents a significant extension to the potential liability of company directors, it is important to ensure that their company's system for the calculation and payment of National Insurance contributions is effective and works efficiently.

6.2 Civil liability

The case of *The Thomas Saunders Partnership v Harvey*, heard in 1989, serves to indicate how the judiciary can draw aside the corporate veil of limited liability when directors have failed to exercise an adequate degree of skill and care. In this case, a recommendation from the director as to the suitability of certain materials for a particular job was contained in a letter to the plaintiffs on the company's headed notepaper, bearing the director's reference and signed on his behalf by his wife, the only other director. The materials subsequently failed and the plaintiffs claimed damages from the director personally on the grounds that he had been negligent when making the recommendation on behalf of his company. The court held that the director was personally liable for the advice given, and that representations made on company headed notepaper could be regarded as representations of the individual director, and not merely of the company.

Being a small family-controlled company, the service offered by the company – and its main asset – effectively comprised the skill and expertise of the husband, its primary director and principal shareholder .

A more recent case, *Williams v Natural Life Health Foods*, was decided finally in the House of Lords in 1998 and this appears to amend slightly the reasoning followed in the Thomas Saunders case.

In this instance, an aggrieved franchisee, Williams, sued both the franchiser company (then in insolvent liquidation) and its managing director, alleging that he had been persuaded to take on the franchise based on representations regarding the business experience and expertise of the franchiser's managing director. Financial projections prepared at the direction of the managing director forecast high initial profits, but in fact a substantial loss was incurred by the plaintiff. Both at first instance and in the Court of Appeal, it was held that the managing director was personally liable for Williams' loss on the grounds that he held himself out to have the relevant business experience upon which Williams could rely, and that he gave express directions regarding the preparation of the financial projections.

However, in the Lords it was decided that to establish a director's personal liability, there had to be an assumption of responsibility by the director that created a special relationship between the customer and the director. Although, in this case, the director owned and controlled the company and the company held itself out as having the relevant expertise derived from the director's own experience, their Lordships did not regard these circumstances as sufficient to make the managing director personally liable. In particular, there had been no conduct of the director to suggest that he was willing to assume personal responsibility to the customer, nor any evidence that he had ever met Williams or discussed the investment plans with him.

Notwithstanding this reprieve directors, particularly of small companies, should ensure that any advice given is clearly and diligently provided in the name of the company, in order to minimise the risk of a director being held personally liable should it subsequently turn out that the advice given was incorrect.

In *Re D'Jan of London Limited* the liquidator brought a summons against a former director on the grounds that he had been negligent in completing and signing a proposal form for fire insurance, with the results that the insurers had repudiated liability for a fire at the company's premises which destroyed stock to the value of £174,000. The director accepted that the form had been completed incorrectly but claimed in his defence that he had not filled in the form himself or even read it before he had signed it. The court held that the director was liable to compensate the company for the loss caused by his breach of duty as he had clearly been negligent, and it was no defence to argue that because he held 99 per cent of the shares (his wife held the other 1 per cent) the shareholders would have ratified the director's action if they had known about the mistake.

In the Court's view, the breach of duty in failing to read the form before signing was not gross and was apparently the kind of thing that could happen to any busy man! The only people whose interests he was foreseeably putting at risk by not reading the form were himself and his wife. The director had acted honestly and therefore, for the purpose of obtaining relief under section 727 of the Companies Act, he acted reasonably and should be excused from some, but not all, of the liability that he would otherwise have incurred. The court declared that the director was liable to compensate the company for the loss suffered by forfeiting his right to the unpaid dividends in the liquidation to which he would have been entitled as an unsecured creditor. This emphasises once again, that the Court now expects the director who fails to exercise proper due skill and care to provide a measure of compensation to the company for the loss suffered.

6.2.1 Directors and unpaid creditors

Third party claims on directors are most often made by unpaid creditors and the Insolvency Act has strengthened their position by the introduction of the offence of wrongful trading. This is in addition to the existing criminal sanctions imposed by the Companies Act on directors who are found guilty of trading with the intent to defraud creditors, i.e., fraudulent trading.

Wrongful trading extends the ambit of risk for directors. The court has the power to make directors personally liable for the debts of a company which is in insolvent liquidation and cannot pay its debts in full, including contingent and prospective liabilities. Where the court is satisified that at some time before the company went into liquidation, the director knew, or ought to have known, that there was no reasonable prospect that the company could avoid insolvent liquidation, then it may order the director to make an appropriate contribution to the company's assets. No limit is set on the amount and the only defence is that the director took all possible steps to minimise the creditors' potential loss once aware that liquidation was inevitable. What constitutes 'all possible steps' will vary with the facts, and will depend on the interpretation of the courts, as the legislation gives no guidance.

If the directors are judged to have acted recklessly or incompetently, with detrimental consequences for the creditors, ignorance of the company's true financial position is no longer a defence when ascertaining the conclusions that ought to have been drawn.

It should also be remembered that non-executive, shadow and nominee directors, as well as those working full-time for the company, have a joint and several contingent liability and should therefore ensure that they are aware of the company's day-to-day financial position, referring if necessary to professional advisers, and reviewing the position by reference to management accounts and records.

Details of some of the wrongful trading actions to come to court are given in **Chapter 8**.

6.3 Criminal liability

Misappropriation of company assets and trading with intent to defraud creditors has long been punishable in the criminal courts. A director personally involved in a transaction by which the company obtains property, or a pecuniary advantage by deception, or where there is false accounting, may be fined and/or imprisoned. As well as a fine and/or imprisonment, negligence or dishonesty, and an active involvement with a company carrying on business for a fraudulent purpose – or continuing to trade and incur debts without a reasonable prospect of the creditors being paid – may bring personal liability for all the company's debts.

Criminal proceedings can also be brought for offences under the general law, for instance, under the Road Traffic Acts 1960 to 1991, if the company is using an unsafe vehicle. Usually the company will be fined, but responsibility may be laid at the director's door and the director may have to account to the company in cash or in kind and again face a fine and/or imprisonment.

Other offences under the general law, for instance under the Trade Descriptions Act, bring 'strict' – that is, automatic – liability; it is not necessary to prove intention and conviction follows if an offence is proved. The general law, of course, applies to any business and in the past directors, unless personally involved, have normally been protected by limited liability unlike the proprietor of an unincorporated business. However, there are now several statutes, e.g., the health and safety or environmental legislation, where directors can be personally liable for fines and penalties imposed by the courts.

6.3.1 Corporate killing

It has been widely accepted for some years that the law on corporate manslaughter is in need of reform. In order to obtain a successful conviction for manslaughter, the prosecution must show that the defendant either knew or was grossly negligent as to the consequences of his action. Where the defendant is a company, that knowledge must be imputed to an individual within the company, i.e., a director or other senior officer who is proved to possess it. Therefore, it is much easier to bring a successful prosecution against a small company where there are short lines of responsibility, than against a larger one.

For example, the small company (and its managing director), which organised a canoe expedition in Lyme Bay where four teenagers drowned, were successfully prosecuted, whereas the prosecutions brought against P&O European Ferries after the Herald of Free Enterprise disaster at Zebrugge, and against Great Western Trains and its senior officers after the Southall rail crash in 1997, both failed. In the latter cases it was not possible to show to the satisfaction of the court 'that senior management had sufficient detailed knowledge of the circumstances to prove the guilt of any single individual'.

However, despite the proposal for change put forward by the Law Commission in 1996 and the consultation paper published by the Home Office in May 2000 (*Reforming the Law on Involuntary Manslaughter: The Government's Proposals*), the law has not yet been amended.

The proposals in the consultation paper envisage that the offence of involuntary manslaughter would be replaced by three new offences – corporate killing, reckless killing and killing by gross carelessness. This would allow companies to be prosecuted for collective management failure, rather than having to prove an individual was responsible, where:

(a) management failure by the company is the cause of, or one of the causes of the person's death; and
(b) that failure constitutes conduct falling far below what can be reasonably expected of the company in the circumstances.

The most serious of these offences, reckless killing, would carry a maximum sentence of life imprisonment if a person can be shown to have been aware that their conduct would cause death or serious injury.

The consultation paper concludes that further consideration should be given to a number of issues, including:

- extending liability for management failure to a parent or group company, if appropriate;
- making company directors personally liable if they contributed to the management failure with a penalty of imprisonment in separate criminal proceedings;
- disqualifying any individual who was shown to have had some influence on, or responsibility for, the management failure causing the person's death, from acting in a management role in a company or business.

The objective of these proposals is to make it easier for companies and their officers to be prosecuted successfully. Whether the tragic accidents on the railways at Hatfield in 2001 and at Potters Bar in 2002 will provide the impetus for the necessary amendments in the law to be included in the Government's legislative programme remains to be seen.

6.4 Disqualification

Directors have always been personally at risk if the company runs into financial difficulties, but the Insolvency Act extended their exposure. All directors, whether full-time, or independent, non-executive, shadow or de facto, are potentially at risk. The responsible and honest director, however, is still protected by limited liability – always provided the director has carried out the requisite statutory obligations, although this may require expert guidance and support.

6.4.1 The Company Directors Disqualification Act 1986

Directors can be disqualified for offences under the Companies Act:

(a) on conviction for an offence connected with the promotion, formation, management or liquidation of the company;
(b) in a winding up, if the company continued to trade with intent to defraud creditors;
(c) if guilty of fraud in relation to the company;
(d) if there has been non-compliance with the directors' obligations under the Companies Act. There must, however, have been 'persistent default', that is, there must have been at least three offences within five years, so comparatively minor offences can bring a disastrous penalty. Application for an order is by any of the current shareholders, creditors, the Secretary of State for Trade and Industry, or the person administering an insolvent company's affairs. The delinquent director can be disqualified from acting as director of a company or being involved in company management (directly or indirectly) without the leave of the court for up to 15 years.

For offences under the Companies Act the court has a discretion whether or not to make a disqualification order, but historically an order has only been made after very blatent breaches of duties by directors.

6.4.2 Disqualification after investigation

The Secretary of State for Trade and Industry is also permitted to apply to the court where he is led to believe, from a report made by Inspectors appointed under either the Companies Act or the Financial Services Act, that it is in the public interest that a director be disqualified.

Re Samuel Sherman plc, heard in 1991, was the first application brought in these circumstances and involved the conduct of the sole director of a public limited company, where the business was run down, the assets liquidated, and the share quotation suspended. Had the company been put into liquidation at this stage, there could have been a substantial return to shareholders. However, the director then entered into transactions which were not only *ultra vires* but also resulted in many breaches of statutory provisions and ignored both the wishes of the shareholders and warnings from the company's auditors. Matters were only brought to a head by the intervention of the Registrar of Companies and the DTI. As the company was not insolvent the court had discretion as to whether a disqualification order should be made, even though it was satisfied that the director's conduct rendered him unfit to be concerned in the management of a company. However, the director was disqualified for five years, the court taking a serious view of any breaches by a director of a public company of statutory provisions which had been established to protect the investing public.

6.4.3 Insolvent companies

Under the Company Directors Disqualification Act the court has to make an order to disqualify directors of insolvent companies if particular circumstances occur and certain conduct is proved to its satisfaction. Once the facts are proved, it has no discretion.

The application to the court for a disqualification order is made by the Secretary of State, or in a winding up by the court, by the Official Receiver. This follows the submission of a report on the conduct of the directors from the office holder administering the insolvent company's affairs, or from the Department of Trade and Industry after an investigation under the Companies Act.

The Company Directors Disqualification Act requires the court to decide whether the director's conduct of the company, alone or in conjunction with any conduct as director of another company, makes the director unfit to be concerned in the management of a company. It sets out guidelines as to what should be considered in making an order. The list is not intended to be exhaustive and, rather surprisingly, there is no requirement at present under the Act for the court to take account of the director's general commercial dealings. The matters listed are:

(a) misfeasance or breach of fiduciary or other duty to the company;
(b) misappropriation, retention of assets or any conduct giving rise to an obligation to account to the company;
(c) the extent of the director's responsibility for company transactions at an undervalue, thereby prejudicing the interests of creditors (these include gifts, whether or not made in consideration of marriage, as well as transactions at considerably less than market value);
(d) the extent of the director's responsibility for a failure to maintain proper accounting records or proper statutory books and the failure to prepare and approve annual accounts.

If the company is insolvent, the court must, in addition, assess the director's responsibility for:

(a) the causes of insolvency;
(b) the company's failure to supply goods and services for which whole or part payment has been made;
(c) voidable transactions (that is, those that can be set aside) with third parties made at an undervalue or giving preference to particular creditors

or transactions made with the intention of putting assets beyond the reach of the company;

(d) failure to call creditors' meetings or to deliver the 'statement of affairs' (setting out the company's financial position) required in a liquidation.

Some acts involve an element of fraud which must be proved, but if creditors are prejudiced, an intention to defraud need not be proved. Disqualification is for a minimum of 2 and a maximum of 15 years, unless the court consents to amend the order. This topic is further examined in **Chapter 8**.

6.4.4 Acting while disqualified

The Secretary of State maintains a Register of Disqualification Orders which is open to public inspection on payment of a fee, and anyone acting while disqualified is jointly and severally liable with the company employing them for debts incurred during the period of disqualification. The liability extends to anyone acting on the instructions of someone disqualified, so that, for instance, disqualified persons cannot appoint their spouse to act on their behalf.

6.4.5 Disqualification and Competition Law

A provision in The Enterprise Bill, if it becomes law, will enable courts to disqualify a director of a company which has been found to have committed any breach of competition law, if the court considers his conduct as a director makes him unfit to be concerned in the management of a company. As drafted, the provisions give the courts extensive powers. There is concern that this could give rise to disproportionate sanctions being imposed, and hence there is significant opposition to this particular proposal.

6.4.6 Trading under the same name

Anyone who was a director, or shadow director, of a company at any time within 12 months of its going into insolvent liquidation may not, except with the court's leave, be either a director or concerned in the management of another company using the same or a similar name for a period of five years. Anyone contravening this is liable to a fine or imprisonment.

By way of example, in 1997 three former company directors were found guilty of being directors of East Africa Lines Limited. This was a company with a prohibited name since all three had previously been directors of a company called East Africa Freight Lines Limited which had run into financial difficulties and gone into liquidation. The directors were sentenced to 200 hours community service and disqualified for two years.

6.4.7 Directors' and officers' liability insurance

The natural reaction of a director who finds himself involved in proceedings arising from acts committed in his capacity as a director of a company is to look to that company for an indemnity in respect of that liability and those costs. Indeed, if the director were astute, he may already have had the foresight to have negotiated an indemnity from his company, having checked the company's articles and the provisions of s310 of the Companies Act 1985 to ensure it had the power to grant such indemnities.

The extent to which a director is entitled to look to his company for an indemnity has been governed by the Companies Act since the 1929 Act. Whilst a company is prohibited from giving a director wide-ranging protection, a company is not prevented from purchasing and maintaining insurance cover on behalf of its directors. Such insurance varies in scope depending on the particular 'D & O' policy purchased. Most, however, do not protect the director in respect of claims brought against them by or on behalf of the company.

It is a common misconception that companies are entitled to cover under the 'D & O' policy in their own right. In fact, the company is only entitled to be reimbursed any monies paid out to the directors and officers by way of indemnification – not even any costs incurred by the company in defending itself are covered. Thus when considering whether to purchase 'D & O' cover, it is essential for directors to take advice regarding the definition of the terms in order to clarify the items actually covered – for example, the costs of representation at regulatory or other judicial hearings may well not be included in many 'D & O' policies. It is important not to assume automatically that all reasonable losses will be recovered, as the precise phrasing of the insuring clauses differs from policy to policy.

7 Insolvency

The main source of primary legislation relating to insolvency, is the Insolvency Act 1986, which incorporated only some of the recommendations contained in the 1982 Cork Committee Report. However, these included those provisions aimed at making directors of insolvent companies personally accountable for reckless and incompetent management which has jeopardised the interests of creditors.

7.1 Identifying problems

Without regular management information, directors of even the most successful company cannot know whether profits could be increased still further. More importantly, there is always a possibility of an un expected cash flow problem of which they had no warning and for which no provision has been made.

Failure to comply with the requirements of the Companies Act is often indicative of poor management. Potential customers, suppliers and lenders, who usually take up credit references or carry out a company search at Companies House may not wish to do business with an unknown company where the audited accounts filed with the Registrar are significantly in arrears. Historically this was far from uncommon, but the situation has improved in recent years following the imposition upon companies of potentially substantial fines by the Registrar for the late filing of accounts.

Nevertheless, it is still too often the case that companies in financial difficulties have poorly maintained accounting records and, therefore, inadequate financial and management information. Accurate and up-to-date records are never more vital than when the company is under financial pressure. Without them neither the directors nor their advisers can make the right decision: whether it is to eliminate loss-making activities or products, to seek further working capital or to reduce stock in trade and trade debtors to improve the company's cash flow.

Up-to-date financial information and accounts enable the directors to make the decisions, rather than having them imposed from outside, possibly by impatient creditors. Of course, management accounts in themselves serve no useful purpose, unless decisions are made in the light of their contents, but they should provide information from which short-term profit forecasts and cash flow projections can be prepared so that the benefits from future trading can be evaluated, and the likely outcome of any company reorganisation, refinancing or debt rescheduling properly assessed. All aspects of the business must be considered, including its product range, marketing strategy and sale prices.

7.1.1 Options and decisions

When there are cash flow problems, the directors must consider:

(a) taking appropriate corrective action within the company to alleviate the current cash shortage and to generate a cash surplus and subsequent profits;
(b) raising additional equity or loan capital;
(c) a sale or merger with a third party with the financial resources to assist the company over its difficulties.

If the cash position is so critical that future trading is impossible, the directors must either:

(a) reach an informal or voluntary arrangement with creditors in an attempt to solve the company's difficulties; or
(b) enter into one of the formal insolvency procedures.

At a time of financial crisis, the directors must seek outside help and advice, either from their auditors and/or solicitors or from an independent licensed insolvency practitioner, experienced in monitoring and advising companies in these situations.

7.2 When is a company insolvent?

Insolvency can bring personal liability to the directors but the first problem is to determine whether the company is, in fact, insolvent.

Unfortunately, there is no precise legal definition of insolvency, although a company would be regarded as insolvent under the Insolvency Act if either it is unable to pay its debts and discharge its liabilities as and when they fall due, or the value of its assets is less than its liabilities. When determining a company's liabilities, contingent and prospective liabilities must be taken into account, as well as actual and quantified amounts.

Even then, unfortunately, it is possible for the company's assets to exceed liabilities and yet for it still to be insolvent; for instance, the company may have purchased a freehold property for investment purposes and have no cash available to pay salaries or the electricity bill. Additional finance can probably be raised on the security of the property but, until this is done, technically the company is insolvent.

The requirement that contingent and prospective liabilities be taken into account was introduced by the Insolvency Act, and its implication may be far-reaching, as there is usually a very substantial difference between the company's financial position as a going concern and assessment on a break-up basis when contingent, or prospective, liabilities crystallise and must be brought into account. A simple example is contained in **Chapter 9**.

7.2.1 Insolvency and directors

Directors have formerly continued to trade, and may still be tempted to, without proper regard to contingent liabilities or future agreed liabilities, for example under credit agreements, on the basis that as immediate cash problems recede so will contingent liabilities. Prior to the Insolvency Act, one judge had held the view that there was 'nothing wrong' in the directors obtaining credit when they knew that the company could not meet its liabilities as they fell due, provided business was not carried on in such a manner that it was clear that the company never would be able to satisfy its creditors. If the directors genuinely believed prosperity would return, then it may have been permissible to incur credit to get over the bad times. However, in the light of the provisions of the Insolvency Act, the courts may take a different view as demonstrated by some of the cases discussed in the next chapter. What has become clear from judgements made in recent years, is that the courts will not tolerate conduct by directors who are complacent, simply believing that their problems will magically disappear, or who are reckless, having no regard for the interests of creditors.

If there is any doubt as to the company's viability and the directors are contemplating taking on further debt, perhaps by increasing the company's bank overdraft, they must take professional and expert advice, not least for their own protection.

For instance, without the necessary guidance, the directors might be liable for:

(a) issuing cheques when it should have been clear that there were no funds to meet them. If the company is at the limit of its overdraft facility, the bank should be informed to avoid if possible any potential personal liability falling on the directors, as well as to prevent one dishonoured cheque precipitating disaster;

(b) any loss to the company arising from disposals of assets at undervalue. If, for example, in order to raise funds quickly, assets are sold off at prices below their reasonable market value, then the company could turn to those involved for reimbursement of the loss;
(c) permitting a supplier to recover stock already delivered, and to which they have not retained title with the intention of reducing the company's liabilities. This may amount to a preference favouring one creditor over the others – the transaction can then be set aside and the creditor required to return the goods unless all creditors are paid;
(d) wrongful trading, by allowing the company to continue to trade, to the detriment of the creditors, when they should have known that insolvent liquidation was inevitable.

The message for directors is clear: take proper professional advice. The pressure of financial problems often makes it difficult to make objective decisions, particularly if the directors have personally guaranteed the company's debts. If the directors have to seek assistance, whether from bankers, suppliers or customers, they are likely to have a more sympathetic hearing if all the facts and financial details are available. If valuable time is lost in collating information and seeking advice, impatient creditors may take precipitate action, possibly leading to liquidation, which might have been avoided if the necessary information had been readily to hand.

7.2.2 Cash management

More often than not in these circumstances, the most important element of financial information required, in the short term at least, when directors are attempting to work out a survival strategy going forward, is a cashflow projection. Depending upon how critical the cash position is, this should be prepared on a weekly or even a daily basis, for the following three to 12 months. Where the cash situation is projected to be difficult for only a relatively short period before improving, it may well be possible to trade out of the crisis if the funds available are properly managed. To do this effectively, it is important to control suppliers' and other creditors' expectations about when they will be paid, by preparing and agreeing with them a realistic payment plan which stands a fair chance of being adhered to. Of course, this can only be done if the company has a reasonable grasp about when cash is going to be received from debtors. Therefore, regular dialogue with both customers and creditors is a must. No one likes last minute surprises – in the majority of cases, creditors will listen to and try to accommodate arrangements for deferred payment terms where they can and perhaps even more importantly, where they believe the company is being open and even-handed with all creditors.

7.2.3 Acting in the interests of the creditors

The greater the likelihood of the company failing at some point in the future, the more important it is for directors to act in the interests of the creditors, in priority to those of the shareholders. Where, in the opinion of the directors, continued trading is likely to mitigate, or even avoid creditors' losses, then the directors are justified in doing this, although for their own protection, they should seek the advice of a licensed insolvency practitioner at this time.

Responsible professional advisers have been giving this advice to their clients for years, and would undoubtedly support the Review Group's recommendation that their proposed schedule of general principles for directors, which highlights this particular issue, be incorporated into company law.

Directors should ensure that precise and detailed minutes are taken of all board meetings from the moment that they are aware that the company's viability is in question. The directors need to be able to demonstrate that they acted responsibly and in accordance with professional advice, with the intention of minimising any potential loss to creditors. If this is done, but unfortunately the company subsequently fails, they are less likely to be found personally liable for any losses arising.

7.2.4 Institute of Directors' guidelines

The gist of the recommendations issued by the Institute of Directors in their publications is as follows:

(a) Directors of a company must at all times have up-to-date and accurate financial information, and, should this point to financial difficulties, take action with all speed.
(b) Directors of a company in financial difficulties should seek competent professional advice.
(c) Directors are entitled to consider, and obtain advice upon, whether it is feasible for a company to secure a moratorium with its creditors to enable it to attempt to resolve its problems without recourse to formal insolvency procedures.
(d) If an insolvency proceeding is inevitable, the directors should attempt to effect it as soon as appropriate.

Directors should have a broad knowledge of formal insolvency procedures, not just because their own business might at some time be at risk, but also because they may wish to instigate proceedings against customers who will not, or cannot, pay the company. This knowledge may also be useful if the company has incurred a bad debt and an aggrieved creditor wishes to have the company's affairs investigated. In addition, should the worst occur, directors do have certain continuing responsibilities after formal insolvency procedures have started.

7.3 The present insolvency regime

In the present insolvency regime, there are three principal procedures available for saving businesses and companies.

7.3.1 Company voluntary arrangements

Under this procedure, a company in financial difficulty can put proposals to its creditors which are likely to involve either a moratorium period or a compromise whereby creditors agree to accept less than 100 pence in the pound on their outstanding debts. If approved by the requisite majority (75 per cent or more in value) of creditors the arrangement, which is subject to the supervision of a licensed insolvency practitioner, is binding upon all creditors who had notice of the meeting. This is the only UK corporate insolvency procedure under which the control of the company's trading activities remains with the existing management, albeit subject to external supervision.

However, under the law as it currently stands, the company has no protection from any actions creditors may take to recover their debts in the period before the creditors' meeting to consider the proposed arrangement. Neither are the directors protected from any subsequent claim against them for wrongful trading. As a result of this uncertainty there have been a relatively small number of company voluntary arrangements attempted since 1986.

In 1993 the Government set up a working party to examine the reform of the law relating to company voluntary arrangements (CVA). A number of deficiencies had been identified during the recession of 1991–1993 and there was concern that the two new procedures introduced by the Insolvency Act, CVA and administration, both of which were intended to assist with the rescue of companies and businesses in difficulty, had been little used. On the other hand, the number of receivership appointments had risen exponentially, although receivers appointed at that time had found few buyers for the businesses they were attempting to sell. As a consequence, many businesses were closed down, thousands of jobs were lost and substantial losses were incurred by both the appointing banks and other creditors generally.

Following the working party's review, the DTI proposed a procedure to enable directors of small companies in financial difficulties to obtain a moratorium which would prevent creditors from taking action against the company or its property for a period of 28 days. The objective is to give the company's management a breathing space within which to formulate a proposal for a CVA to put to creditors for their approval. The relevant legislation was subsequently incorporated into the Insolvency Act 2000, although the enabling provisions have yet to be approved by Parliament. When these come into force, directors of small companies, as defined in the Companies Act will be able to secure a moratorium by simply filing certain documents in court. The documents must include the terms of the proposal, and be supported by a report from a licensed insolvency practitioner agreeing to act as nominee in the period prior to the creditors' meeting convened to consider the proposal.

7.3.2 Receivership

When the company's banking or other credit facilities are secured by a debenture issued by the company, giving the lender a charge over its assets, the lender can usually enforce the security by appointing an administrative receiver ('the receiver') under the terms of the debenture deed. The directors can ask the debenture holder to make the appointment, and the lender, normally the company's bankers, will usually agree to this if the appointment is likely to maximise the recoveries from the sale of the company's assets.

The receiver

The receiver acts as agent of the company and his primary function is to realise the assets covered by the charge for the benefit of the debenture holder, subject to the prior claims (if any) of other creditors secured by a fixed charge ranking ahead of the debenture holder and to the claims of preferential creditors. Proceeds from the sale of assets covered by a fixed charge are, however, paid to the debenture holder without prior deduction, other than the costs of realisation, and the receiver's fees.

Creditors' claims

Preferential creditors have the first claim against a company's assets covered by a floating charge, so that their claims must be agreed and settled out of the proceeds from those assets before any payment is made to the debenture holder. As at June 2002, preferential creditors include:

- amounts payable to the Crown for PAYE and VAT due for 12 and six month periods respectively, prior to the appointment of the receiver;
- employee claims for arrears of wages up to £800, and for any unpaid holiday pay subject to statutory limits.

However, if the Enterprise Bill becomes law as currently drafted, claims from the Crown will no longer be afforded preferential status. This would be the same for all insolvency proceedings.

Insolvency

The receiver is not empowered to deal with unsecured creditors' claims, and any surplus after payment to the debenture holder and preferential creditors should be returned to the directors for distribution. This seldom arises in practice, as the company has by then usually been put into liquidation and the surplus is paid over to the liquidator for distribution.

Directors and receivers

Once the receiver is appointed, the directors' powers to deal with the secured property are suspended. The receiver immediately appraises the company's financial position, unless this has been done prior to the appointment, and then decides how best to realise the assets of the business. Wherever possible a receiver will attempt to sell a business as a going concern, because this is likely to maximise realisations and may also preserve at least some of the employees' jobs. While dealing as humanely as possible with the employees, the receiver's first duty is nevertheless to the debenture holder who made the appointment.

The directors must prepare a 'statement of the company's affairs' as at the date of the receiver's appointment, setting out full details of the company's assets, debts and liabilities, to be submitted to the receiver within 21 days of receiving the requisite notice from the receiver. They must also give the receiver every assistance.

Directors' service contracts and all other contracts of employment are unaffected by the appointment of the receiver, so that although the directors ' executive powers are suspended, they remain in office and are entitled to payment until the receiver terminates their contract. The directors' other legal powers and duties continue, so they are able to deal with matters not the concern of the receiver, such as registration of share transfers, filing annual returns and continuing legal actions brought by or against the company (but are not likely to have access to company funds to do so).

7.3.3 Administration

Administration is a court driven procedure which provides an opportunity for the directors, the company or the creditors to initiate an insolvency procedure comparable, in certain respects, to administrative receivership where no debenture has been issued. The court will not make an administration order unless satisfied that the company is insolvent and that the administrator is likely to achieve one or more of the following purposes:

(a) help all or part of the company or its undertaking to survive as a going concern; or
(b) enable the company to come to an arrangement with its creditors whether by way of a CVA or through a more formal scheme of arrangement under the Companies Act;

(c) secure a more advantageous realisation of assets for the benefit of creditors than would be likely in a liquidation.

If administration is contemplated the directors should always seek expert advice as to whether application should be made to the court, as they have a duty to minimise losses to creditors once it is clear that the company is insolvent.

A practical issue to solve initially, particularly for small financially distressed companies, is to find the money for the cost of obtaining the administration order. Due largely to the involvement and requirements of the court, this can be significant, which has sometimes meant that administration is simply too expensive for small companies.

Assuming that problem can be overcome, the prospective administrator has to establish how the administration and the conduct of the business during the period of administration are to be financed. Although an administrator is not personally responsible for liabilities incurred by the company during the period of administration, an administrator is obliged to pay for the company's continued use of assets belonging to third parties e.g., leased premises or plant etc. Therefore, before making an administration order, the court will require to be satisfied the company has sufficient funds to finance the ongoing business. Banks are generally less willing to lend to administrators than they are to administrative receivers whom they have appointed themselves. Thus administrations are more likely to succeed when the business generates cash takings regularly – football clubs and retailers are good examples – as opposed to those which have substantial working capital needs, requiring the administrator to borrow significant sums to enable the business to continue.

The administrator

Whilst the administrator's powers are very similar to those of the receiver, as an officer of the court he owes a duty of care to all the company's creditors, whereas a receiver's primary duty is to his appointor only, the debenture holder. However, an administrator can resist the claims of secured creditors more effectively than a receiver so there are circumstances when it may be advantageous for the directors to seek the appointment of an administrator rather than an administrative receiver. These would include:

(a) when a significant part of the assets employed in the business are either leased or are on a hire purchase agreements; or
(b) when there are a number of potentially disruptive claims by creditors who seek to recover assets used in the business as the goods were supplied under terms of trading which included a retention of title clause; or

(c) if there are licence agreements or other contracts which would be liable to forfeiture upon liquidation; or
(d) if there are material overseas assets. Being appointed by the court, an administrator may be able to establish his legal authority in overseas countries more easily than an administrative receiver.

Within three months of appointment, the administrator must submit his proposals for the conduct of the administration to creditors for approval. Once approved, he then monitors the management of the company's affairs in accordance with the terms of the proposal, subject to the supervision of the court. For more urgent decisions, he is entitled to apply to the court for sanction.

However, an administrator has no power to deal with the company's creditors, and therefore, once the scheme has been successfully implemented, any distribution to creditors will have to be made by either a liquidator, or by the supervisor in a voluntary arrangement.

Directors and administrators
The directors have the same obligations to an administrator as they have to a receiver; that is, they must submit a statement of affairs within 21 days of receiving the requisite notice from the administrator and supply any information required.

7.4 The 'rescue culture'

The 'business' as opposed to 'company' rescue procedures under the insolvency regime as it exists in July 2002, are administration and administrative receivership. These two procedures provide the office holder appointed an opportunity, where appropriate, to continue a company's trading with a view to selling the business and assets as a going concern. Hopefully, with new management and funding being made available, a viable business will emerge, but the corporate entity of the failed company does not survive, unless administration has been used as a prelude to a CVA, but it is the latter process which preserves the corporate entity. The sale proceeds are distributed to the creditors in accordance with their priority under the Insolvency Act, but in recent years with many more of a company's assets being subject to third party finance, the unsecured trade creditors have rarely received any significant repayment of their debts.

Nevertheless, the political drive to find ways of supporting companies more effectively than in the early 1990's remains strong and as a consequence, further changes to our insolvency procedures have been included in the Enterprise Bill, which is making its way through Parliament as this edition is being written. The comments on the Enterprise Bill that follow are based on the Bill as it stood at June 2002, and therefore may not be correct should there be further amendments before it becomes law.

7.4.1 The Enterprise Bill

The Enterprise Bill currently before Parliament which, together with the associated new Insolvency Rules, is likely to be enacted in its final form during 2003, contains a number of reforms to the existing insolvency law.

The holders of newly created floating charges will not be able to appoint administrative receivers

Whereas administration is regarded as an inclusive procedure, operating in the interests of the creditors generally, as noted earlier an administrative receiver's primary duty is solely to his appointor, the holder of a floating charge. Under the terms of the debenture, in specified circumstances the floating charge holder is empowered to appoint a receiver, irrespective of the wishes of other creditors ranking after the floating charge holder, or of the shareholders.

This is no longer regarded as acceptable and therefore, apart from a few particular exceptions contained in the Enterprise Bill, the holders of newly created floating charges will not be able to appoint an administrative receiver. However, in order to protect the interests of secured creditors, it is proposed that the holders of floating charges will be allowed to appoint an administrator of their own choice without the need to apply to court. Further, should the company seek to make an appointment independently, the directors will still need to give five days notice of this to the secured creditor, who will then have the right to apply to court to appoint their own nominee as administrator instead. Presumably, the intention is to enable the holder of the floating charge to be able to make a quick appointment of the administrator of their choice in times of crisis, but certain changes will need to be made to the procedure proposed, if the administrator is to be as effective as a receiver can be now.

Nevertheless, administrative receiverships will still continue for some years yet, as holders of floating charges which pre-date the proposed legislation will still be able to appoint receivers under their existing charges.

The purpose of administration is fundamentally changed

As presently drafted, an administrator's primary objective will be to attempt the rescue of the company, as opposed to the whole of part of the company's undertaking or business. If this is not considered to be reasonably practical, then the administrator is to seek a better result for creditors than would be likely if the company went into liquidation. If this fails, the property of the company is to be sold by the administrator who will be able to make a distribution to secured and preferential creditors.

When exercising his duties the administrator will be required to act in the interests of the creditors as a whole. Therefore he should ensure that if he decides that the only viable option is to sell the company's assets for the benefit of the secured or preferential creditors, the decision is carefully thought through and well documented as it may be challenged by a disgruntled creditor.

The setting of priorities in the way the Bill is presently drafted is likely to create a number of practical difficulties for the administrator. For example, it may only be possible to preserve the corporate entity if the creditors agree to a significant write-off of their debt – but in this situation, creditors could well receive a better return from the sale of the business and undertaking rather than from an attempt to continue within the existing company structure. Hence the administrator could have an inherent conflict between his responsibilities to try and preserve the company, and to act in the best interests of the creditors.

As a consequence, these proposals have given rise to considerable concern because a critical factor in the successful rescue of many financially distressed companies is the speed with which a sale of the business as a going concern can be achieved. As soon as it becomes public knowledge that a company is in financial difficulties, key employees and customers are likely to take action to protect their longer term interests by taking their custom elsewhere. The longer the period of uncertainty, the greater the probability that the business will fragment, thereby severely damaging the chances of an administrator selling the business as a going concern. Therefore the requirement under the Enterprise Bill as currently drafted, that an administrator must give priority to selling the corporate entity, which will certainly be more problematic and hence time consuming, if not impossible, may significantly reduce the prospects of preserving businesses and jobs. This is of course, completely contrary to the government's objectives.

It is to be hoped that the government will listen to these widespread concerns, with the result that the Bill will be amended to allow an administrator greater flexibility to act in the way which he believes will produce the best result for the creditors. Such a change would be welcome as directors of troubled companies are then more likely to seek advice at an earlier stage, consequently enhancing the prospects for the revival of their company's fortunes.

Another change proposed is that the timescale within which the administration is to be concluded is likely to be set at one year – there is no time limit at present. The administrator's proposals are to be sent to creditors within 8 weeks (as opposed to three months now) ahead of a meeting to consider them, which must be held two weeks later. Although application can be made to court to extend these timescales, in the opinion of those people specialising in helping distressed companies, the time limits proposed are ambitious for all but the simplest cases. Therefore administrators may find themselves needing to return to court for further extensions, which will increase costs.

Therefore if the government's prime objective of promoting 'Business Rescue' is to be fulfilled, it is essential that the advantages of speed and flexibility afforded to a receiver remain available in fast-track administration.

Improved returns for unsecured creditors
It is hoped this will be achieved in two ways:

(a) the preferential status of government creditors will be abolished;
(b) a proportion of the funds released by the abolition of Crown preference is to be earmarked for the benefit of unsecured creditors. Exactly how this will work is not yet clear. This proposal echoes the recommendation made by the *Cork Committee* in 1982, to retain 10 per cent of floating charge realisations for distribution to unsecured creditors. However, unless the sum of money retained for distribution is reasonably significant, there is a danger that most of the fund will be absorbed by the costs of agreeing creditors' claims.

7.4.2 Summary

One of the principal objectives behind the changes proposed is the promotion of 'company rescue' by making the process more inclusive for all creditors. As noted earlier, it is no longer regarded as acceptable that one creditor can take action to enforce their security without any regard to the interests of other creditors.

7.5 Liquidation

If the directors have no choice but to stop trading, the possibility of selling the business as a going concern is probably remote.

In these circumstances a debenture holder may well not want to appoint a receiver but prefer to claim repayment as a secured creditor in the liquidation, as the debenture holder's security is not thereby prejudiced.

If there are no grounds for appointing an administrator, the directors should take expert advice from a licensed insolvency practitioner as to whether the company should go into voluntary liquidation.

7.5.1 Directors' responsibilities prior to liquidation

The directors are in a difficult position during the period between the board meeting at which they decide that the company should be put into voluntary liquidation and the relevant statutory meetings of shareholders and creditors. Until formal appointment of a liquidator, the company remains under the directors' control, even though the insolvency practitioner to be nominated as liquidator by the shareholders will normally be advising the directors.

Statutory duties
In a voluntary liquidation, a liquidator can usually be appointed far more quickly than in a winding up by the court. The directors have a duty to creditors to implement the decision as quickly as possible, in order to avoid any possible dissipation of the assets prior to appointment of the liquidator, although there may be no option but to let the company be wound up by the court, despite the further delays this entails, if a valid resolution of the shareholders cannot be passed or the directors themselves cannot agree.

Preserving the assets
Prior to the appointment of a liquidator, the directors can only:

(a) dispose of perishable and other goods likely to diminish in value if they are not immediately sold; and
(b) do anything necessary for the protection of the company's assets.

Protecting the assets may involve considerably more than simply locking up and vacating the company's premises. Necessary action involves subjective decisions, and the directors should therefore consult with the insolvency practitioner before taking action. Broadly, however, they should:

(a) only retain employees if their presence is necessary to protect the assets, or they can enhance the assets' value – for example, by converting work in progress into saleable products;
(b) ensure the assets are secure and not disposed of prior to appointment of the liquidator; requests by leasing and hire purchase companies to remove their goods should be resisted and referred to the prospective liquidator;

(c) take any decisions relating to the conversion of work in progress into finished products after professional advice, as the goods may be subject to a retention of title clause. Creditors attempting to repossess goods on this ground should be referred to the prospective liquidator; this is a technical area, and the liquidator must decide whether the clause is legally effective;

(d) pay cash received into a new account opened specifically for the purpose with a bank which is not the company's bank. A separate account should be opened even if the company's bankers hold a fixed charge over book debts, as the liquidator will pay over the monies collected when the validity of the charge is confirmed. Failure to open a separate account may amount to a preference favouring the bank at the expense of other creditors – although the directors may be tempted to reduce the overdraft in an attempt to mitigate their liability where they have given personal guarantees to the bank for the company's facilities;

(e) freeze the company's old bank account and cancel standing orders and direct debits. Payments should be from funds in the new bank account and should only be made if they are essential for the preservation of the assets; for instance, if non-payment of an electricity bill would result in deterioration of a company's trading stock of frozen food, payment would normally be justified;

(f) make cash payments for goods and services required, as at this stage directors may be personally liable for discharging any credit incurred by the company before the liquidator is appointed.

7.5.2 Voluntary liquidation

Voluntary liquidation is instigated by a special or extraordinary resolution of the shareholders requiring a straight majority or three-quarters majority vote respectively. If the company is solvent, a members' (that is, shareholders) voluntary liquidation can be agreed by special resolution, but an insolvent company must be placed into a creditors' voluntary liquidation, requiring approval of an extraordinary resolution. The liquidator's appointment as 'office holder' commences on the date of the resolution.

The shareholders usually appoint the liquidator, but the appointment must be confirmed at the creditors' meeting when the creditors can also appoint a liquidation committee to protect their interests and assist the liquidator.

The Insolvency Act states that the creditors' meeting must be held within 14 days of the shareholders' meeting and the creditors must receive at least seven days' notice of the meeting. Notices advertising the meeting must also be placed in the London Gazette and in two newspapers local to the company's principal place of business, giving either the name and address of the insolvency practitioner advising the directors or an address nearby where a list of creditors can be inspected for two working days prior to the meeting. If there has been more than one place of business, notices and lists must be issued for each location, but if the company has no place of business in Great Britain, the list must be available at the registered office.

The statement of affairs must be verified by affidavit and presented to the creditors' meeting by the directors and should include assets, debts, liabilities and a list of the names and addresses of creditors.

One of the board is appointed to chair the creditors' meeting and the directors should attend to report and answer questions. This is the only time creditors can question the directors and very often they take full advantage of the opportunity. Both the company and its directors can be fined for non-compliance with the regulations relating to creditors' meetings.

7.5.3 Directors and liquidators

Once the liquidator is appointed, the directors' powers cease, although in a creditors' voluntary liquidation, the liquidation committee or the creditors in general meeting may authorise them to take specific action.

During the winding up the directors must assist the liquidator, providing any information and documentation requested. If they do not co-operate, the liquidator can ask the court to order the directors and officers to produce an account of their dealings with the company and all relevant documentation. The order can require the directors to be examined under oath and the court can also order seizure of company property and relevant documentation held by the directors and anyone involved in the promotion, formation, trade, dealings, affairs or property of the company; failure to comply with the orders may result in imprisonment.

7.5.4 The liquidator

The liquidator's principal duties are:

(a) to take possession of the company's property – title does not vest in the liquidator, although the liquidator has custody of the assets;
(b) to realise the assets for the benefit of creditors. In order to obtain the maximum for the creditors, the liquidator may have to bring proceedings to recover the company's property which has been misappropriated or sold at an undervalue. If the court is satisfied that the company paid over cash or released assets to creditors within six months of the liquidation with an intention to prefer one creditor over other creditors, the transaction may be set aside as a preference. If, however, the preferred creditor was connected with the company at the time, inten-

tion is assumed and the six-month period is extended to two years. Payments made to the company's bank may also come under this head, but the liquidator must satisfy the court that there was an intention to prefer the bank as a creditor by reducing the company's overdraft as against all other creditors. This may not be difficult where the directors have personally guaranteed the overdraft and/or no other creditors have been paid;

(c) to agree the creditors' claims and distribute the assets realised to the secured, preferential and unsecured creditors. Essentially, payment can only be made to the unsecured creditors after creditors secured by either fixed or floating charges, and after the costs of realisation and the preferential creditors have been paid in full. Any surplus remaining after payment of all costs and creditors is distributed to the shareholders.

In addition, the liquidator must investigate the company's affairs and the conduct of its officers. In a winding up by the court, these are the duties of the official receiver.

7.6 Reports on the conduct of directors

The Insolvency Act places a specific duty on the administrative receiver, the administrator, the liquidator of an insolvent company, or, in a winding up by the court, the official receiver – that is, the office holder – to submit a report to the Secretary of State on the directors' conduct.

The format of the report is set out in the Insolvent Companies (Reports on Conduct of Directors) Rules 1996 which require reports to be submitted by office holders within six months after the commencement of the relevant insolvency proceedings.

The report must include:

(a) details of all individuals who have been directors within three years prior to insolvency, including non-executive and shadow directors, their names, addresses and period of service;
(b) their position in the company;
(c) remuneration voted and received, together with cash expenses and benefits in kind;
(d) a list of other directorships, including shadow and non-executive directorships during the three years prior to receivership or liquidation;
(e) details of any other companies with which the directors were associated which may be relevant to the consideration of the directors' conduct;
(f) any other matters which should be considered;
(g) a summary of the company's statement of affairs;
(h) details of connected companies with which the company had dealings.

Clearly the report calls for a thorough investigation in relation to the insolvent company as well as any other connected companies with which the directors have been associated.

When submitting their reports, office holders have to decide whether the conduct of individuals involved in the company's affairs has been such that they should be regarded as either de facto or shadow directors. The Disqualification Unit of the Insolvency Service has issued guidelines as to the information it wants office holders to provide when submitting reports, and these are very helpful when assessing whether a person has acted as a shadow director:

(a) was he a signatory to the company's bank account?
(b) did he place purchase orders for goods and services on behalf of the company?
(c) did he sign contracts on behalf of the company?
(d) did he attend board meetings regularly?
(e) in what capacity did the individual deal with employees, customers or creditors?
(f) is he an essential source of information for the office holder about the company's affairs?

Obviously each case needs to be assessed on its own merits, but if a significant number of these questions apply then the individual concerned must be at risk of being regarded as at least a shadow director and hence having his conduct reported upon.

Primary responsibility for applying to the court for a disqualifaction order, based on the report, rests with the Secretary of State, but in certain circumstances the official receiver may be directed to do so; however, the delinquent director can call evidence to rebut the allegations. The court must be satisfied that the directors' conduct may make them unfit to be concerned in company management. If disqualification is ordered, the period of disqualification only starts to run 21 days after the date of the order, unless the court provides otherwise.

It should be emphasised, however, that the minister who took the Insolvency Bill through Parliament stated that he was not seeking to condemn the unsuccessful entrepreneur. In his view, 'Insolvency is a fact of life, but it is clearly the time to consider how the directors have discharged their duties and responsibilities'.

7.7 Directors' personal guarantees

Directors' personal guarantees only become liabilities when the company cannot pay its debts. However, as new companies without a track record can rarely obtain credit or finance facilities without these being underwritten by the directors, they should be aware of the risks involved.

7.7.1 Bank guarantees

A personal guarantee of the company's bank overdraft is probably the most common undertaking given by directors in support of the company and is often backed up by a charge on the director's home. If so, the bank will usually require the director's spouse to be a joint and several guarantor, in order to improve their security, as the bank's charge then takes priority to the spouse's claim to the equity in the property.

For the bank's charge to be effective against the borrower's spouse, the spouse must be separately advised by an independent solicitor. If the correct procedure is not followed, the bank's right to enforce its security against the spouse's interest in the property may be challenged on the grounds that the bank's customer, the principal borrower, exerted 'undue influence' over the spouse to sign the charge documents.

Directors should try to resist requests for charges over personal assets, particularly in the case of their house, as any charge given for business purposes by one spouse, but agreed to by husband and wife, removes the protection given under the general law to the owners. Most clearing banks will ask for a debenture giving them a fixed and floating charge over the company's assets as security for the bank's overdraft, and if the directors have given personal guarantees, they should suggest this, rather than charging their own property. However, a debenture issued in respect of indebtedness already incurred may not provide effective security for up to 12 months, depending on the nature of the charge and whether any new money has been provided since issue of the debenture. Accordingly, independent legal advice should always be taken before entering into any agreement to guarantee the company's overdraft or charge either the company's or a director's personal assets.

Under a debenture agreement granting fixed and floating charges over the company's assets, the lender is entitled to repayment in two tranches if there is default:

(a) firstly, out of assets covered by the fixed charge (in priority over other creditors); and
(b) secondly, out of the proceeds of sale of the assets covered by the floating charge, subject to the claims of the preferential creditors.

For many years, the majority of clearing bank debentures have given the lender a fixed charge over their customers' book debts and hence first call on the debt or monies should the borrower become insolvent. However, in June 2001, the Privy Council in *Re Brumark Investments Ltd* held that unless the bank exercised truly 'effective control' over the proceeds of book debts when paid into the company's bank account, the bank's charge could only be regarded as 'floating' as far as book debts were concerned.

Consequently, upon the customer's insolvency, the debtor monies will be available to pay the claims of preferential creditors ahead of the bank. If the claims of the preferential creditors are substantial, then the bank may well recover significantly less from the company, which will result in much larger claims being made against the guarantors.

Therefore, where directors have given personal guarantees to their company's bankers, it is in their own interests to ensure that the company's banking arrangements are such that the company can only use book debt collections with the bank's specific consent. Where the Bank's control is regarded as adequate, then the bank will still have first claim against these monies under a fixed charge; legal advice is obviously essential to get this right.

If the debenture charging the company's assets as security is backed by the directors' personal guarantees, the lender can claim repayment from either the company or the guarantors, although of course it cannot claim in total more than it is owed. In practice, banks usually wait for a distribution from the company's assets to creditors before seeking to recover any shortfall from guarantors, although they are not obliged to do so under the terms of the standard agreements used by most clearing banks.

If the directors provide personal guarantees initially, and the company expands so that its net asset value is substantially increased, it may be possible to persuade the company's bank to agree to release the director's personal guarantees as the charge on the company's assets may represent sufficient security.

7.7.2 Business leases

Landlords frequently require directors to guarantee a company's obligations under a lease, particularly as it is often very difficult to sell a leasehold interest in industrial or commercial property. If the lease cannot be assigned reasonably quickly in a winding up, the liquidator can disclaim it as onerous, leaving the landlord with an unsecured claim in the liquidation for the company's obligations under the lease, including any claim for dilapidations, which may be substantial. When the directors are sureties, that is, guarantors, of the company's obligations, the landlord can turn to them for payment. Even if the lease is assigned, the directors' obligations as sureties will normally continue until either the lease expires or the landlord consents to their release. The directors may therefore find themselves liable for the acts and omissions of a third party for a considerable period after the company has vacated the premises.

7.7.3 Hire purchase and leasing agreements

Finance companies often ask directors to underwrite their company's obligations under these agreements. If, for any reason, the agreement is terminated prematurely, the balance of instalments due and payable for the whole period is usually payable immediately. The lender can of course look to the directors for repayment of the full amount if the company cannot do so (less a deduction for the resale value of the property leased).

8 Insolvency and Director Disqualification

8.1 Disqualification orders

The Company Directors' Disqualification Act 1986 provides that where a company is insolvent, and a director's conduct is found to warrant disqualification, the court has no discretion – it must make a disqualification order. Following a substantial increase in the resources committed to the Director Disqualification Unit in 1994/95, the number of disqualification orders obtained by the Secretary of State has risen sharply since then as the table below shows.

Table 5: **Disqualification orders**

	Company liquidations[1]	*Disqualification orders*[2]
1988	10,842	263
1989	12,311	274
1990	20,309	278
1991	30,167	306
1992	24,425	409
1993	20,708	497
1994	16,728	399
1995	14,536	392
1996	13,461	727
1997	12,610	1,040
1998	13,203	1,267
1999	14,280	1,284
2000	14,317	1,540
2001	14,972	1,548
2002	N/A	1,761

[1] Year to 31 December.

[2] Year to 31 March.

Source : Department of Trade and Industry

However, the number of directors who have been disqualified is still a tiny proportion of the total number of directors of failed companies. In addition there is real concern that there appears to be no procedure in place to check that disqualified directors are not continuing to be involved in the management of companies in breach of the terms of the disqualification order. This concern is reinforced by the fact that a significant number of directors appear to be involved in the failure of more than one company.

As part of the Government's campaign against cowboy directors, an informer's telephone line was launched in January 1998, which can be used by anyone having dealings with a company where they believe a director is either already disqualified or is an undischarged bankrupt. The Register of Disqualification Orders is also available for inspection on the Internet.

8.1.1 Protection of the public

The principal objective of the disqualification procedure remains the protection of the public, as set out in the following extract from Sir Browne Wilkinson's remarks in an early case heard in March 1988:

> 'The primary purpose of disqualification is not to punish the individual, but to protect the public against the future conduct of companies by persons whose past records as directors of insolvent companies have shown them to be a danger to creditors and others. Ordinary commercial misjudgement is in itself not sufficient to justify disqualification. A balanced view is required to be taken of directors' conduct. In isolation, technical offences such as the failure to lodge annual returns or to maintain adequate statutory records will not warrant disqualification.'

The growth in the number of disqualification cases now commenced by the Secretary of State has been a deliberate policy. Civil disqualification proceedings are now seen as the most visible method of enforcing the law relating to directors and their obligations. Through general deterrence, the process of disqualification aims at encouraging other directors to behave properly thereby improving the standards of commercial morality throughout the business community. Lord Woolf, MR, endorsed this approach in *Re Westmid Packing Services Ltd, SSTI* v *Griffiths*, when he said that disqualification is not just about keeping 'bad' directors 'off the road' but also seeks to protect the public by deterring the disqualified director and by encouraging other directors to behave well.

8.2 The grounds for disqualification

The approach of the court when dealing with the disqualification of directors of insolvent companies has consistently followed the fundamental principles established in the most cases heard in the late 1980s which had regard to the factors in Schedule 1 of CDDA. The judgments in the cases referred to in this chapter have clarified and identified:

(a) those transgressions by directors which warrent disqualification;
(b) the appropriate period of disqualification that particular categories of wrong doing by directors merit; and
(c) those individuals involved in the management and control of a company who should be disqualified.

8.2.1 Unfit conduct

It is unlikely that the court will take a damning view the first time a company fails unless there has also been serious misconduct by the directors – in a capitalist society, we should all be allowed one mistake. Nor are isolated, technical defaults likely to result in disqualification, but there are certain occurrences which the courts will view seriously and regard as potential grounds for disqualification. These include:

(a) phoenix companies;
(b) arrears of Crown debts;
(c) excessive benefits to directors;
(d) inadequate accounts and accounting records;
(e) misappropriation of company assets, or trust funds;
(f) failure to cooperate with the office holder or the court;
(g) trading whilst insolvent.

8.2.2 Phoenix companies

A common feature of 'the phoenix company syndrome', is that an insolvent business has been continued by means of a succession of limited companies which operate from the same premises, use the same plant and machinery and, very often, are controlled by the same directors. Frequently there is inadequate equity capital to finance the second or third revival properly. This means that directors of the successor business run the risk of being prosecuted for wrongful trading if it is clear that there was never any real prospect of the business being able to trade profitably and, hence, insolvent liquidation was inevitable.

In the case of *Re Ipcon Fashions Limited*, which was wound up in 1986, the director had carried on business in the clothing trade for some 15 years, through various companies, three of which had gone into insolvent liquidation in 1977, 1980 and 1985. He had failed to introduce any capital into his successive ventures and had traded at the risk of his suppliers, his bankers and the Crown. During the four months prior to liquidation, the director transferred the business to a new company yet continued to draw a salary for himself and his wife. In the view of the judge, the director had shown a reckless disregard for the interests of all the creditors and, hence, was disqualified for five years.

8.2.3 Arrears of Crown debts

Perhaps not surprisingly, another common feature of insolvent companies, and sometimes even of solvent ones, is that the payment of debts due to the Crown – notably monies deducted for PAYE and VAT – is in arrears. In the case of *Re Stanford Services Limited* (1987), the judge considered there was a practical difference between Crown debts, and debts owing to ordinary trade creditors. It was accepted that most trading companies rely, to some extent at least, on credit from suppliers of materials, goods and services and, as such, the occasional bad debt is regarded as a normal commercial risk. The Crown, however, has to be viewed as an involuntary creditor; employers must deduct PAYE and National Insurance contributions from their employees' wages and salaries and, although these contributions are not strictly trust monies, non-payment not only prejudices the Crown but may also have an adverse effect on those employees. In the opinion of the judge, by allowing this situation to continue, directors could be personally liable on two counts:

(a) they were acting improperly by failing to keep themselves informed, with reasonable accuracy, of the company's financial position, and, as a result, trading was carried on with monies which ought not to be used to finance the company's current trade;
(b) they were continuing to trade at a time when they ought to have known that the company was unable to meet its current and accruing liabilities.

On the second count, not only could the directors be disqualified, but they could also be held personally liable to contribute to the company in liquidation should a liquidator bring an action for wrongful trading. In fact, in this particular case, the disqualification order was made for two years only, due to certain other mitigating circumstances.

Directors who allow debts to the Crown to accumulate significantly will be at risk should their company collapse. In these circumstances, courts may well consider directors to be more culpable if they fail to pay Crown debts (using the money saved to finance the continuation of an insolvent company's business) than if they fail to pay commercial debts, although this approach was qualified to some extent by the *Re Sevenoaks Stationers* case referred to in **8.2.6**.

8.2.4 Excessive remuneration

Unpaid creditors have always shown anger at meetings of creditors when it appears that the directors have continued to pay themselves either excessive remuneration or other benefits at a time when their company was unable to pay its trade creditors. On the basis of the case of *Re DF Limited* (1987), this point will also be taken into account by the courts. The company had gone into liquidation owing substantial sums to the Crown in respect of PAYE, National Insurance and VAT. Although the director owned the premises from which the company operated, rent was paid to an associated company, also owned by him. The court held that the levels, both of rent paid and of remuneration voted to the director, were excessive and operated to the detriment of creditors, and therefore made a disqualification order for four years.

This case underlines the need for directors to be circumspect when drawing remuneration, should their company be experiencing cash flow problems. In principle, directors should only pay themselves what the company can reasonably afford.

8.2.5 Accounts and accounting records

The importance of accurate and up-to-date accounting records has already been stressed, since directors are unable to fulfil their obligations without them. Obviously the courts do not expect all directors to have a detailed technical knowledge of accountancy, but it is clear that the courts do expect them to be aware of the company's financial situation and of the obligations imposed upon the board by the Companies Act.

In the case of *Re Rolus Properties Ltd and Another* (1988), application for the disqualification of the director was made on the grounds that as a director of two companies – both of which were in liquidation – he had not only failed to maintain any books of account for an extensive period, if at all, but had also failed to file returns with the Registrar of Companies and to prepare audited accounts. As a chartered secretary had been the secretary of one company and a director of the other, it was felt that this mitigated the respondent's culpability and the director was only disqualified for two years. Nevertheless, the judge ruled that, although in this instance the absence of books appeared to be a matter of incompetence rather than dishonesty, it demonstrated that the director was not fit to hold office because of his lack of understanding of paperwork. He should, therefore, in the future, be kept off the limited company scene for the protection of the public.

In the case of *Re Majestic Recording Studios Ltd and others*, heard in March 1988, the director concerned had previously been involved in three insolvent companies, one of which had been wound up without ever having filed either accounts or annual returns. The director claimed in his defence that he had no concern in or control over any financial matters and did not know why accounts and returns had not been filed. For this reason he pleaded that no disqualification order should be made. In disqualifying him for three years, the judge took a different view, stating that, as director, his duties did not allow him to leave these matters to other people, and that the public was entitled to be protected against someone who had done just that.

In the same case, an application for a disqualification order was made against another director of the same three companies. Whilst he offered no defence in respect of his conduct of the affairs of the three companies in question, he requested leave to continue as a director of an unrelated company which appeared to be trading profitably, was maintaining regular records and was preparing audited accounts. Although this director was disqualified for five years, his request was granted, in that he was permitted to retain his directorship of that company only, on condition that an independent chartered accountant, approved by the court, was willing to act as a co-director with him and that audited accounts were filed within 14 months of the end of the accounting period.

These decisions emphasise the collective responsibility directors have to monitor the company's financial position at regular intervals and to ensure that the company's accounting records enable them to do so effectively. Although the task of maintaining the necessary records can be delegated to others, the ultimate responsibility remains with all directors, and is one which cannot be abdicated with impunity.

Nevertheless, in *Re Cladrose Limited*, applications had been submitted to disqualify two respondents as company directors on a number of grounds, which included, for all three companies concerned, the total failure to produce either audited accounts or to file any annual returns. However, no disqualification order was made against the first director as he had submitted in evidence that he had relied upon his co-director, a qualified accountant, to produce the accounts.

8.2.6 Period of disqualification

The most important case in this respect is *Re Sevenoaks Stationers (Retail) Limited*, heard in the Court of Appeal in July 1990 after a chartered accountant had been disqualified for seven years following the liquidation of five companies of which he was one of two directors. When reducing the period of disqualification to five years, the court set out guidelines as regards the seriousness of offences, which have been generally followed in subsequent cases:

(a) the top bracket of disqualification for periods over ten years should be reserved for particularly serious cases, for instance, where a person fell to be disqualified for a second time;
(b) the minimum bracket of two to five years should be applied where the case was not very serious; and
(c) the middle bracket of six to ten years should be applied to serious cases which did not merit the top bracket.

In the *Sevenoaks* case the director concerned, although there were some mitigating circumstances and he was not actually dishonest, had acted either incompetently or negligently to a very marked degree which was sufficient to render him unfit. There were substantial debts due to the Crown, and the accounting records were totally inadequate so that the relevant returns to the Registrar had not been made. As a chartered accountant, many of these deficiencies were his direct responsibility and it was accepted that his period of disqualification should be longer than that of his fellow director who had neither a professional qualification nor financial expertise. However, the Court took note that following the failure of these companies, the director concerned had suffered very greatly – he had lost a substantial sum of money personally and had drawn only modest, if any, remuneration. Thus, the Court felt it was not appropriate that the period of disqualification should be more than double that of his fellow director who had been disqualified for three years, so that the period of disqualification was reduced from seven to five years.

The attitude of the courts to the arrears of Crown debts was also refined in this case, in that the judge stated that because a company was effectively the Crown's appointed collector for both PAYE deductions and VAT, the non-payment of any Crown debt should not be regarded *automatically* as evidence of a director's unfitness. It is then necessary to look more closely at each particular case to see what significance, if any, the non-payment of the Crown debt has.

Therefore, when considering the appropriate period for disqualification, the courts will have regard to mitigating factors which may include:

- acting upon professional advice;
- the employment of an appropriately qualified person;
- reliance on regular management information and forecasts;
- personal financial commitment or loss;
- failure caused by external factors outside the director's control.

8.2.7 De facto directors

In another case, *Re Cargo Agency Ltd*, a deficiency of some £225,000 had accrued by the time the company went into liquidation in May 1988 after some 16 months of trading. Management accounts prepared in August 1987 after only eight months showed the company to have been insolvent and, in the court's opinion, a reasonable director would have ceased trading at that time. A balance sheet as at 31 January 1988 was subsequently prepared for a prospective purchaser and this showed that the company was still insolvent with the result that the directors took preliminary steps to put the company into liquidation. However, by the time the liquidation commenced some four months later, debts had increased by a further £40,000. Mrs Keeling was a director, and her husband was a *de facto* director who had subscribed £10,000 for ordinary shares, representing 50 per cent of the issued capital. Although Mr Keeling had risked and lost his own money, his own salary was unreasonably high and the public at large had suffered by the continued trading when no reasonable person could properly have done so.

As the case was not regarded as serious, the judge disqualified the respondents for two years, and gave leave for Mr Keeling to be engaged in the management of another company for which he was then working. However, there were two mitigating factors:

(a) the directors had lost £10–£20,000 of their own money;
(b) the directors' reliance upon the other shareholder, a substantial company, for the provision of accounting services.

In another family company, *Re M O'Donnell & Sons (Huddersfield) Ltd*, mother, father and son were disqualified for three, eight and seven years respectively. The son, John, strongly defended the Secretary of State's application claiming that he had not been formally appointed a director. However, the court found that John, acting jointly with his father, had played an increasingly significant role in the management of the company and for at least five months prior to liquidation, he had assumed the status of director, and had acted as a *de facto* director.

The judge also disqualified the mother, Mrs Anne O'Donnell, on the grounds that she had abrogated her responsibility as a director, because by her own admission, she had taken no part in the management of the company, and had left everything to her husband and son – not an uncommon situation in a family business!

8.2.8 Standard of competence

This concern in the courts over the need for directors to understand their obligations as directors was again emphasised in *Re Ameron Limited* (1997), where the directors were found to have committed most of the mortal sins, namely to have:

- continued trading for 21 months beyond the point at which they should have known there was no reasonable prospect of avoiding insolvent liquidation;
- made loans to an associated company on a non-commercial basis;
- preferred trade creditors and themselves to the Crown; and
- permitted the company to make excessive payments to themselves.

The directors were each disqualified for three years as the court concluded that although there was no dishonesty on the part of the directors, they simply failed completely to understand their duties as directors.

In a second case, *Re City Investment Centres Limited*, a director was disqualified for ten years; his catalogue of misdemeanours included the acquisition of the trade of another company without having sufficient capital to finance the new business. Both the other directors were also disqualified, in one case because the director had displayed a 'woeful ignorance of the duties concerned attaching to the office of company director'.

These examples should serve as a warning that the courts are not prepared to accept that either ignorance of a director's duties or inadequate commercial experience, both frequent reasons for inactivity, are reasonable excuses for directors failing to fulfil their obligations. Therefore, unless individuals have an understanding of what is expected of them, they should not accept appointment as directors without first taking proper advice regarding the obligations involved.

The professionally qualified director

The courts have regularly upheld the principle that the degree of skill and care required to be executed by a director will be much higher for a professionally qualified person than for others. Two particularly pertinent examples involve professionally qualified individuals who acted as nominee directors when providing off-shore company formation services.

The first case, *SSTI* v *Solly* heard in the Court of Appeal in 1998, involved a company which had gone into voluntary liquidation just over a year after incorporation, with a deficiency for the unsecured creditors of over £1.6m.

The director concerned was a chartered accountant who made his living by holding numerous 'nominee' directorships through a company owned by his wife and himself. In his defence of the proceedings brought by the SSTI he had claimed that he was not a director and was firmly of the opinion that he was not one, despite having consented unconditionally, in writing, to become a director of the company, and had charged for his services through his own company. His admitted total inactivity in the performance of any of the duties of a non-executive director of the company was consistent with that belief.

However, the Court of Appeal held that Mr Solly's honest belief that he was not a director was not reasonable and was not a defence to the Secretary of State's charge. He was a professional man who made his living by holding nominee directorships.

The fact that he had taken on over 1000 directorships, and as a result could not remember them all, did not release him from his inescapable personal responsibilities. In the court's view, his inactivity and total abrogation of responsibility contributed, in significant measure, to the continuation of the very serious malpractices of the other directors for as long as they did, and hence he should be disqualified for three years.

In a not dissimilar, but much more serious case, *Re Vass and Anor*, involving a company, Oldham Vehicle Contracts Ltd, (OVC) which operated a car rental business from premises in Manchester, London and Stanstead Airport, Mr Crowshaw, a resident of Sark, was disqualified for 12 years, having totally neglected his duties and responsibilities as a director of OVC and of other specified companies. At that time he was recorded as having 1313 appointments as a director of UK companies. He had agreed to act as nominee director as part of his business of supplying nominee director services and his terms of engagement for these companies stated, inter alia, that:

- he would have no involvement in the management or running of the company; and
- he would act only on the instructions of the appointor, without making any, or any substantial, independent contribution or enquiries;
- his role would essentially be restricted to signing forms and filing documents.

The court accepted the report of the Official Receiver, that by agreeing to act on these terms, it inevitably meant that the nominee director could not exercise any reasonable degree of supervision or control over the conduct of the company's affairs.

The court was not prepared to tolerate a situation such as this, where somebody by way of business, takes on the directorship of so many companies whilst abrogating any responsibility for how the companies are run. The court therefore intended that the period of disqualification for Mr Crowshaw should act as a deterrent to others who may be engaged in similar activities.

8.2.9 Allocation of responsibility

Other cases also underline the need for directors to exercise proper diligence in the conduct of their duties, even when relying on more senior or expert colleagues on the board. Where appropriate, the courts will seek to allocate responsibility between directors for the company's failure and vary the period of disqualification accordingly.

In *Re Austinsuite Furniture Limited* disqualification orders were successfully sought against all three directors. The managing director, who was disqualified for seven years, was judged to have acted irresponsibly, and demonstrated both a lack of understanding of the duties of a director and an unwillingness to discharge these duties.

One of his more junior colleagues was disqualified because the judge considered him to have been irresponsible in accepting a director's appointment without any commercial experience. However, having done so he had to accept responsibility for the management of the companies.

8.2.10 Delegation and supervision

At the other end of the scale, in *re Barings plc (No 5)* Mr Tuckey, the deputy chairman of the Barings Group, was disqualified because he failed to ensure that the affairs of Barings Futures (Singapore) Pty Ltd ('BFS'), were ever properly investigated despite the known difficulties in relation to funding, the known lack of controls and the known warning signs. The collapse of the Barings Group in February 1995, resulting in administration orders being made in relation to those companies in the group, was directly attributable to the unauthorised trading of a single trader, Nick Leeson, in Singapore. The key question raised by the judge was why his trading activities were allowed to continue for so long, undetected and uncontrolled.

Barings Group Management Structure

The management structure within the Barings Group consisted primarily of various managerial committees – as a consequence the statutory boards of directors of companies within the group performed a more limited function. Thus the board of Barings plc met relatively infrequently. In Mr Tuckey's view, the Barings' system of management permitted a high degree of delegation and decentralisation and wherever possible responsibility was delegated downwards. However, it was not the Bank's practice to interrogate senior members of management as to what steps had been taken to maintain effective control of the business.

Mr Tuckey normally spent as much as 80 per cent of his time on client work, and hence given the importance of his ability to win business for the group, there had to be a structure beneath him within the organisation which recognised the fact that his management role represented only a small part of his working time.

At the time the crisis in Singapore broke, Mr Tuckey was engaged in advising Wellcome on the defence of a hostile takeover bid from Glaxo which had necessitated him freeing himself from every other responsibility that he could.

Nevertheless he remained chairman of both Barings Investment Bank, and of another key management committee within the Barings Group. The managerial duties required of him in these capacities were not any less because he had other roles to play and therefore had less time to devote to management. In the opinion of the court, it remained incumbent upon him to ensure that there was a proper measure of supervision and control exercised in relation to delegated management functions.

The issues in Singapore

(a) Segregation of duties

As general manager in Singapore, Nick Leeson was in day-to-day control both of BFS's trading activities, and also of its administrative activities, i.e., its back office. He was BFS's head trader and was also in charge of the paperwork, including the recording and settling of trades. BFS was effectively a one-man band; the one man was Leeson.

It is an elementary and fundamental precaution in any business involving trading in securities or financial instruments of any kind that no one individual should be in a position where he can both conduct and settle trades. The story of the collapse of Barings is a classic – and tragic – example of what can happen if this elementary precaution is not taken. It would appear that at all times until he left Singapore in February 1995, Leeson was allowed to remain in the position where he could both conduct and settle trades at BFS; and this despite the fact that an Internal Audit Report had been completed in October 1994, specifically drawing attention to the need to 'segregate' Leeson's trading role from his settlement role.

Although it was accepted by the court that it was not Mr Tuckey's duty personally to ensure that Leeson's roles were segregated, the judge concluded that had he played the positive management role which his duties and responsibilities required him to, the non-segregation of Leeson's roles would inevitably have come to his attention.

(b) BFS reported profitability

Mr Tuckey did not perform or cause to be performed any examination of BFS's profitability despite the fact that during 1994 and 1995 the profits earned by BFS had become increasingly dominant in the group. Such enquiries as were made were purely superficial; the exceptional revenues reported in January 1995 were not questioned. In failing to look into these matters properly, the court found Mr Tuckey to have been in breach of his management duties.

(c) Monitoring of Leeson's activities and other related issues
The court was of the view that Mr Tuckey had effectively abdicated his management responsibility for BFS in favour of other senior executives. He also showed a woefully inadequate understanding of how Leeson's trading operations were supposed to operate. As such, Mr Tucker's purported discharge of his management responsibilities fell well below what was required,

When seeking disqualification orders against three senior directors, the Secretary of State made no challenge of any kind to the honesty and integrity of the respondents. However, the judge considered that had Mr Tuckey and his fellow directors undertaken any steps to satisfy themselves of the true position, they would have been aware that all was far from well. Mr Tuckey's breaches of duty were regarded as a general failure to manage – they amounted not so much to bad management as non-management, and hence Mr Tuckey must be judged as unfit to be concerned in the management of a company within the meaning of the CDDA.

This case should serve as a salutary lesson to all directors of substantial companies operating a sophisticated management structure with extended reporting lines. Ten directors were disqualified and a major financial institution collapsed because of basic failures – described by the group's chairman as 'crass' and 'absolute' – of the internal management controls within the group.

8.2.11 Non-executive directors

Other cases have highlighted the need for all directors, including non-executives, to be vigilant and conscientious when undertaking their duties. In *Re Continental Assurance Co. of London plc* (CAL), disqualification proceedings were brought against a non-executive director who was a senior executive of a merchant bank which had made loans to CAL's holding company to enable it to purchase shares in CAL. As the holding company had no assets other than its shareholding in CAL, it could only repay the bank out of dividends received from CAL. However, CAL did not distribute its profits, but instead loaned the monies to the holding company. As a result, these payments were illegal because they were in breach of section 151 of the Companies Act 1985 – which prohibits a company from providing financial assistance to a third party to purchase its own shares.

The court did not accept the director's explanation that he was not aware of the payments being made by CAL to the holding company, but found that he simply failed to appreciate what the responsibilities of a director were in relation to the understanding of a company's financial affairs. In the court's view any competent director in his position would have known what was going on, and hence his conduct constituted serious incompetence or neglect. When making the disqualification order for a period of three years, the judge concluded that 'it was serious for non-executive directors to fail to appreciate the obvious when it was before them'.

8.2.12 Company doctors

Ever since the Insolvency Act 1986 came on to the statute book, there has been considerable concern about the risks for those involved in assisting or advising companies in financial difficulties of being regarded as 'shadow directors'. As such they have the same potential liabilities as the formally appointed directors. 'Company doctors', in particular, have to be careful to avoid liability for wrongful trading, and given their acknowledged level of expertise, the courts will expect a correspondingly higher degree of skill to be exercised by them. It is therefore important that the contractual basis upon which the company doctor is retained ensures that his services are provided solely as a professional adviser. To that end it must be clear that the board of directors still retains the final responsibility for the management of the company's affairs. Thus, the company doctor must put his recommendations to the board in the form of advice upon which the directors will base their own decisions, rather than as instructions to the board which have to be followed.

Although in *Re Tasbian Limited (No.3)*, a case heard in 1992 by the Court of Appeal, the issue before the Court was not whether the appellant had acted as a shadow director, the judgement provided very useful guidance as to the type of behaviour which would imply that an adviser would be regarded as a shadow director. In this case, an experienced company doctor was appointed as consultant to Tasbian at a time when the company had accumulated losses of £800,000 after three years of trading. On the basis of his advice, additional share capital was subscribed for, a moratorium with major creditors was arranged and the company's employees were hived off to a newly formed shell company which sub-contracted the employees' services back to Tasbian. Eventually the company failed with a deficiency for creditors of £1.4m, the consultant having resigned immediately beforehand. The newly formed subsidiary company also went into liquidation owing substantial sums for PAYE tax and National Insurance contributions.

An application for disqualification of the adviser was submitted on the grounds that he had acted as a shadow director, in that he had:

(a) negotiated the moratorium with creditors, including the Inland Revenue;
(b) monitored the company's trading performance;
(c) become a signatory on the company's bank account and controlled its operation. He determined which of the company's creditors were paid, and in which order, and appeared to exercise a significant degree of control over the company's affairs.

The judge held that in these circumstances there was at least an arguable case that the consultant was either a shadow or a *de facto* director of both Tasbian and the new, hived off company.

Thus, if a consultant acts in such a way that he is actively involved in the conduct of the company's business, his influence being such that the board of directors no longer makes its own decisions, then he is likely to be regarded as a shadow director.

8.2.13 Disqualification and leave to continue to act

Where a director is disqualified he is required to resign all appointments within 21 days of the order coming into effect. To remain as a director of another company, the leave of the court must be obtained. Given that the principal purpose of disqualification is the protection of the public, any application for leave to act as a director of another company will raise the question as to whether the grant of leave is consistent with that. The court has an unfettered discretion to grant leave, and when reaching its decision, will consider a number of factors including:

(a) whether there is a genuine need for either the company, or for the individual, for leave to be granted;
(b) why was the disqualification order made initially? In particular, was the director's unfit conduct attributable to dishonesty and lack of probity, or simply to inadequate management?;
(c) the nature of any defects in company management that led to the disqualification order being made, with a view to assessing whether there is a risk of those defects recurring.

Whilst it is in the public interest for individuals against whom disqualification orders are made to be able to continue to earn their living, the grant of leave to act as a director of a specified company must not undermine the purpose of disqualification orders. The safeguards required will vary according to the circumstances of each case. By way of example, in *Re Gibson Davies Ltd*, heard in the Court of Appeal in 1995, a director was disqualified for five years, but leave was granted to the applicant to continue as a director of another company, after he had offered the court nine separate safeguards. These included:

(1) no cheque or financial agreement to be signed, on behalf of the company, solely by the appellant;
(2) the director's loan account must be subordinated to the claims of all other creditors;
(3) no security over the company's assets to be granted to the director;
(4) all annual returns and accounts to be filed at Companies House within the statutory time limits;
(5) monthly management accounts must be prepared and submitted to the company's auditors. The system of internal accounting control should be improved;
(6) the company's auditors shall report to the board on any matters of concern relating to financial management and, in the absence of appropriate action by the director, report the matter to the Secretary of State.

The court accepted that the appellant could act as a director as long as all conditions were satisfied – when reaching this decision, the court was almost certainly influenced by the contention that the ongoing company was profitable, and that its success was dependent upon the appellant's continued services as a director.

However, once leave has been granted, it is extremely difficult to monitor whether the specific conditions laid down by the court are being met. In the case of Mr Davies, he was disqualified for a second time when the company for which he was first given leave, also went into liquidation.

8.3 Directors' disqualification – and the public interest

In the light of these decisions, some directors might question whether enterprise and the entrepreneurial spirit are now in danger of being stultified by the courts. The Company Directors Disqualification Act imposes a mandatory duty upon the courts to make a disqualification order for a minimum of two years if the court is satisfied that the conduct of a director of an insolvent company makes him or her unfit to act in that capacity. However, the court still retains some discretion in that it must form its own opinion about the director's conduct, and also has the right to permit individuals who are the subject of a disqualification order to act as directors in specific instances.

For example, in the case *Re Bath Glass Limited*, a company which was compulsorily wound up in July 1986 owing significant sums to the Crown, the judge stated that, when assessing a director's conduct, the court must be satisfied that the director was guilty of a serious failure or failures to perform his duties as a director. Whether any failure so to act was deliberate or caused by incompetence was immaterial; any misconduct of the director might be relevant. The courts have to determine whether the interests of the creditors have been prejudiced by the actions of the director and, in doing this, all aspects of a director's conduct must be taken into account.

In *Re Bath Glass Limited*, it was clear that the conduct of the directors could be criticised in certain respects. For instance, during the last 12 months of trading, the company had been under pressure to reduce its bank overdraft. This was only achieved by reducing payments to the Crown. Unless more funds became available, there was a risk that trade creditors would go unpaid. The judge viewed this as improper conduct and a wrong way in which to conduct business.

On the other hand there were mitigating factors including the following :

(a) neither director had acted dishonestly;
(b) neither had benefited personally at the expense of the creditors – in fact they had made a financial commitment to the company themselves;
(c) budgets and sales forecasts were prepared regularly, and with care, albeit they subsequently proved inaccurate;
(d) the directors had taken and acted upon professional advice.

The judge summed up by saying that, although their conduct as directors of Bath Glass had been, in part, both improper and imprudent, he was not satisfied that it had been so serious as to make them unfit to be concerned in the management of a company.

It is evident from this that the court will first examine directors' conduct in relation to the insolvent company and will only examine their conduct in relation to other companies if there is any doubt as regards their fitness to act, or if their conduct in relation to those companies is a matter of complaint. The courts will not undertake a balancing act whereby 'errant' behaviour in respect of one company, whether insolvent or not, is offset by 'good' behaviour in respect of other companies. Disqualification is not intended as a penalty against an individual who is not personally to blame for the fact that a company becomes insolvent even though his or her behaviour may not have been exemplary. The courts are seeking to disqualify those directors who have been either dishonest or grossly negligent, whether that be through recklessness or sheer incompetence.

8.3.1 Carecraft and fast-track disqualification

As the volume of disqualification cases grew during the 1990s, this created pressure on court time, leading to unacceptable delays in the prosecution of cases. These delays were obviously unsatisfactory from both sides' point of view – if the director is found innocent then he wants his reputation to be cleared as quickly as possible, whereas if the charges are proven, the director should be disqualified swiftly in order to protect the public.

In *Re Carecraft Construction Ltd*, the judge sanctioned the use of a summary procedure (the Carecraft procedure) in disqualification proceedings where the facts are agreed and it is accepted by all parties that a period of disqualification is appropriate. The court is then asked to reach its own conclusions – without a full trial – based on the parties' statements and the agreement reached between them. In these circumstances, the judicial process is shortened and the disqualification period is completed more quickly.

Despite the relative success of the Carecraft procedure, judicial support for the introduction of a statutory system of voluntary undertakings where there was agreement between the parties continued to grow in order to save both court time and the parties' costs. The relevant provisions were included in the Insolvency Act 2000, whereby the Secretary of State is now authorised to accept a director's offer of a voluntary undertaking not to be either a director of a company or to be concerned in any way in the management of a company for an agreed period, without the leave of the court. The decision to accept an undertaking is solely within the Secretary of State's administrative discretion where satisfied that the director's conduct makes him unfit and that it is expedient, in the public interest, to accept an undertaking instead of applying to court for a disqualification order.

The incentive for the director to offer a voluntary undertaking, after receipt of a notice advising him that the SSTI intends to bring disqualification proceedings, is that he will not be liable for costs if the offer is made by the director before the SSTI issues proceedings.

The effect of an undertaking is, to all intents and purposes, the same as a court order – the same criminal penalties and personal liability apply as for a breach of an order. The names of persons who have given undertakings are recorded on a public register in the same way as those subject to a disqualification order.

To date, voluntary undertakings have only been accepted where the director has been prepared to admit, or at least not dispute, the reasons for disqualification, which are then recorded in a schedule attached to the published undertaking. However, this practice was challenged on the very first occasion the undertaking procedure was used, (*Blackspur Group plc and*

Eastaway), and although the court of first instance upheld the procedure, the issue is currently subject to appeal.

The simplification of the disqualification procedure through voluntary undertakings may well replace the Carecraft procedure and should also significantly reduce the number of court applications and the delays experienced in hearing disqualification cases.

8.4 Wrongful trading

Considerable publicity was given at the time to the first reported decision involving wrongful trading in which the liquidator of the failed company Produce Marketing Consortium sought a personal contribution of over £100,000 to its assets from the two former directors.

The company had gone into liquidation in October 1987, but its profitability and financial position had been deteriorating for a number of years prior to that. The auditors had qualifed the company's accounts for the year ended 30 September 1984 on the grounds that the company was insolvent at the balance sheet date, although the directors stated that, in their view, the company would be able to trade out of its difficulties. However, turnover fell significantly in the following year, and draft accounts for the two years ended 30 September 1985 and 30 September 1986 were not produced by the auditors until January 1987. These showed that losses had been incurred in both years and that by 30 September 1986 the company had a substantial excess of liabilities over assets, and hence was technically insolvent.

Immediately after the preparation of the accounts, the auditors warned the directors that, in view of past losses and the relatively small profits being forecast, the directors could be found guilty of wrongful trading if trading continued. In the event, the directors did carry on trading until September 1987, without any serious attempt to dissuade the principal supplier (to whom they were eventually left in debt to the sum of £175,000) from continuing to deliver goods. Although the judge emphasised that, in his view, there had been no question of dishonesty on the directors' part, he did regard them as guilty of wrongful trading and ordered them to make a personal contribution of £75,000 to the company's assets. When making his judgment, the judge considered that, in view of the directors' close involvement with the business and the significant fall in turnover in 1985, the directors must have had a pretty shrewd idea that substantial losses were being incurred well before the receipt of draft accounts from the auditors in January 1987. In his view, once the loss for the year ended 30 September 1985 had been incurred, insolvent liquidation was inevitable and the directors did nothing to mitigate the losses to creditors. Once directors recognise that insolvent liquidation is inevitable, such a course of action is likely to be their only defence.

A key point arising from the *Produce Marketing Consortium* case, which should be noted by all directors, is that when assessing the directors' conduct, the judge did not regard their knowledge as being limited by the documentary evidence available to them at the time. In his view, knowledge included all matters which they 'should have found out' given reasonable diligence and a level of general skill appropriate to their experience. Thus the court concluded that the directors were liable to account for losses incurred after July 1986 – being the date by which audited accounts for the previous financial year should have been filed with the Registrar of Companies – rather than from January 1987, when the accounts were first received from the auditors. This represents another example of directors being penalised personally where the company had not complied with its statutory obligations.

Unfortunately, in the *Produce Marketing Constorium* case, no indication was given as to how the contribution of £75,000 to be paid by the directors had been determined. The judgment in *Re Purpoint Limited* was more helpful, despite the fact that the company's accounting records were so incomplete that it was not possible to determine by how much the company's assets had been eroded by the continuation of trading. In fact the judge thought it probable that the company was doomed to failure from the start, given that it had no capital base and the acquisition of its only assets was financed either by bank borrowing or by hire purchase. The business it had inherited had previously been unprofitable, but the director was confident that the introduction of new business would change the situation. Therefore, so the judge believed, it was only fair for the director to be given the benefit of the doubt. However, on the facts before the court, it was clear that by the end of 1986 the company was insolvent, although it did not cease trading finally until November 1987, notwithstanding written advice from the auditors in May 1987 that the company was insolvent. In the absence of any accurate accounts by which the loss incurred could be determined, the directors were ordered to pay an amount equal to the aggregate of the debts owed to trade creditors and the Crown which had been incurred by the company after 1 January 1987.

Despite the success in these two cases, relatively few others concerning wrongful trading have reached court, although the threat of legal action by liquidators has undoubtedly secured a number of contributions from former directors for the benefit of creditors.

In essence, the purpose of assessing wrongful trading as a means of redress is compensatory rather than penal. Directors are liable to pay to the liquidator, by way of compensation to the creditors, an amount which represents the sum by which the company's assets are judged to have been depleted by the directors' reckless conduct in continuing to trade and incur credit at a time when the company was insolvent.

The case of *Brian D Pierson (Contractors) Ltd* re-emphasised, yet again, that all directors, whatever their role in the company, will be held liable if they fail to fulfil their duties properly. In this instance, the two directors, husband and wife, were found guilty of wrongful trading. Although the court acknowledged that the wife had very limited involvement in the company's affairs, she was nonetheless a director. She had seen an auditors' report stating there was fundamental uncertainty about the company's ability to continue trading. By ignoring the warning signs, and having failed to appreciate the questions that ought to have been asked about the company's affairs, the court held she was instrumental in allowing the company to continue to trade, and so liable for wrongful trading.

The case highlights, once more, how essential it is for all directors of even the smallest companies, to be fully conversant with their duties, and to take an active part in the direction of the company's affairs.

When bringing wrongful trading actions to court, a liquidator faces two major difficulties. Firstly, the cost of determining and then pursuing the claim, when often there are limited funds in the liquidation to finance the action. The proposal to allow solicitors to act on a 'contingency fee' basis may alleviate this to a limited extent. Even if a creditor is prepared to finance the action any contribution recovered from the directors is available for the general body of creditors so that the funding creditor is not able to be reimbursed his initial outlay before any distribution is made to creditors. Secondly, the need to be certain that the directors are not men of straw, so that the claim is worth pursuing in the first place.

However, the court's decision against the liquidator in *Re Sherborne Associates Limited*, has made the prospects for a successful action for wrongful trading even more uncertain. Ever since the company started trading, it had consistently failed to reach its projected targets and despite various attempts to turn things around by obtaining new finance and by changes of staff, the company continued to move further into debt. It finally went into liquidation in February 1989. The liquidator brought an action for wrongful trading against the three non-executive directors alleging that after board meetings in January 1988 they should have realised there was no reasonable prospect of the company avoiding insolvent liquidation.

Subsequently the central figure of the three died in 1992 and hence was unable to give evidence and his own explanation of events at the trial, a point which worried the judge when reaching his decision. However, the factors which weighed most heavily in the directors' favour were that the directors were perceived as honest, diligent, well-respected businessmen who had not deceived their creditors. Each one had extensive general business experience and had reached a position of responsibility in other companies.

They had not made any personal gain from the company's operations and apparently kept themselves well informed of what was going on. The judge's decision that the directors were not liable will give liquidators a further reason to pause for thought before commencing wrongful trading claims in the future.

The only defence that directors have under the Insolvency Act, once they are aware of the company's insolvent position, is to take every step to minimise losses to creditors. At this point, the directors' fiduciary duty to the company is enhanced by a statutory duty to protect the interests of the creditors. Therefore, it may not necessarily be sufficient to cease trading and simply put the company into liquidation the instant that problems emerge, albeit that that step ensures no further credit is incurred. There are a variety of formal procedures to be followed once the option arises to close a business down, and therefore to protect themselves the directors need to take independent advice and so be able to make informed decisions as to the route to follow which is likely to be in the best interests of creditors.

9 Directors' unlimited liability – a case study

There is a substantial difference between the valuation of a company's assets valued as a going concern as compared to valuation on a break-up basis. This case study shows how a director can divest himself of the protection of limited liability when he decides, apparently quite reasonably, to take his profit from his profitable trading company, without first taking expert advice.

The estimated balance sheet of Widgets Limited, set out in **Example 1** shows the company with net assets of £66,500 valued as a going concern.

The company has made modest profits for the last few years, after taking into account annual aggregate remuneration for two directors of £50,000. The bank overdraft is fully extended and, as an old established company, the bank have only taken a fixed charge on the company's leasehold premises, supported by the directors' personal guarantees.

One of the company's major customers has become a slow payer over the past 12–18 months and has just gone into liquidation – 20 per cent of Widgets' turnover has therefore disappeared and there is a potential bad debt of about £19,000.

Widgets' managing director is unwell and he decides to call it a day and liquidate his company while he can get some money out: 'Even with a £19,000 bad debt the company is still worth £47,500 after paying off the creditors'.

The liquidator is appointed and meets the following problems.

(a) Widgets' premises are in a light industrial estate where several units are vacant and available to let. As there seems little prospect of assigning the lease, the liquidator, with the bank's agreement, gives notice to the landlord and disclaims the lease on the ground that it is 'onerous'. This leaves the landlord with a claim in the liquidation for £5,000 for dilapidations plus £30,000 for rent; £15,000 of the 'cash' balance represents a rent deposit held by the landlord's solicitors. No funds are realised for the bank.

Example 1: Balance Sheet – Widgets Limited

	£	£
Leasehold improvements		6,000
Plant and machinery		50,000
Motor vehicles		15,000
Computer equipment		25,000
Intellectual property		5,000
		101,000
Less: finance liabilities		(50,000)
		51,000
Current assets		
Debtors	95,000	
Stock	82,500	
VAT refund	10,000	
Cash	15,500	
	203,000	
Current liabilities		
Trade creditors	95,000	
Inland Revenue	30,000	
Bank overdraft	45,000	
Loan – company pension fund	10,000	
Employer/employee pension contributions	7,500	
	187,500	
Net current assets		15,500
Net assets		66,500

(b) The plant and machinery, vehicles and computer equipment in the balance sheet were bought on finance and, after disposal of the assets, £18,000 remains owing under the various agreements.

(c) Further motor vehicles were leased and the leasing company has repossessed them.

(d) Widgets sold manufactured goods with a 12-month warranty clause and also did some contract work. Several debtor accounts represent retention monies and balances held pending completion of maintenance work. As the company can no longer meet warranty claims, customers are seeking compensation, credit notes are issued and so realisations from book debts are anticipated to be only £45,000.

(e) One supplier establishes a valid retention of title claim and recovers stock with a book value of £20,000. A substantial part of the remaining stock consists of spare parts with an estimated resale value of only 20 per cent of cost.

(f) After liquidation, debts due to or from government departments are regarded as claims of the Crown, so debts due from one department are set off against claims by other departments. The refund of VAT due has therefore been set off against the claims of the Inland Revenue and the Department of Social Security for outstanding PAYE and National Insurance deductions.

(g) Unpaid claims by employees against a company that goes into liquidation (or receivership or administration) are paid up to certain limits, directly by the Department of Trade and Industry Redundancy Payments Service. Arrears of salary up to a maximum of £800, and all arrears of holiday pay and pension contributions, rank as preferential claims against the company. All other employee claims, such as pay in lieu of notice and redundancy, are unsecured.

(h) The company's statement of affairs shows pension contributions overdue for sums deducted from employees' wages but not paid over to the pension scheme of £1,500, and £6,000 representing four months pension contributions not paid over by the employer.

(i) The loan from the pension scheme was taken to pay for the registration of a patent; no repayments have been made. It is not uncommon for small companies to use their company pension schemes as a source of non-interest bearing funding when the company's cash flow becomes tight, on the basis that things will improve in the short term, when the loan can be repaid. However, in this case, the patent became worthless due to advances in technology.

After taking into account the costs of realising the assets and of the liquidation and the claims of preferential creditors, there is only a modest sum left for the claims of the unsecured creditors, which are increased on cessation of trading by claims from:

	£
(a) Employees – holiday pay	8,000
(b) The Department of Employment – for the element of redundancy pay normally paid by the company	11,000
(c) The landlord – for dilapidations and rent (net of rent deposit)	20,000
(d) Shortfall due to the finance company	35,000
(e) The leasing company – for the balance of the lease payments, after deducting the sale proceeds of the vehicles	10,000
	84,000

Example 2: Widgets Limited

	Book value £	£	Sums realised £
Leasehold improvements	6,000		–
Plant and machinery	50,000		10,000
Motor vehicles	15,000		12,000
Computer equipment	25,000		10,000
Intellectual property	5,000		Nil
	101,000		32,000
Less: hire purchase liabilities	(50,000)		(50,000)
	51,000		
Shortfall			(18,000)
Current assets			
Debtors	95,000		45,000
Stock	82,500		12,500
VAT refund	10,000		Nil
Cash	15,000		500
	203,000		58,000
Total assets	254,000		
Costs of liquidation			(10,000)
			48,000
Preferential creditors –			
Employees		8,000	
Bank overdraft (wages advanced)		6,000	
Unpaid pension contributions			
– Employer		6,000	
– Employee deductions not paid over		1,500	
			(21,500)
Fund available for the unsecured creditors			26,500
Unsecured creditors –			
Trade, including finance company		78,000	
Bank overdraft		39,000	
Leasing creditor		10,000	
Landlord		20,000	
Department of Employment		11,000	
Loan from company pensions scheme		10,000	
PAYE after set-off of VAT		20,000	
			(188,000)
Deficiency as regards unsecured creditors			(161,500)

The estimated outcome of the liquidation is set out in **Example 2** and is very different from that envisaged by the Managing Director when he decided to call it a day.

The figures speak for themselves; certainly there were better alternatives including:

- the directors could have attempted to sell the business, valued as a going concern, rather than putting it into liquidation; or
- an orderly and planned wind down of the business leading to closure.

What is most worrying, however, is that, under the Insolvency Act, Widgets was technically insolvent – that is, it was unable to pay its debts on the basis that its liabilities exceeded its assets, after taking into account contingent *and* prospective liabilities. These totalled £84,000, more than the company's net asset value as a going concern. Clearly the directors should have taken expert advice before taking action.

The above case study assumes that the changes in legislation incorporated in the Enterprise Bill will be approved, and hence the monies due to the Inland Revenue for PAYE and National Insurance contributions deductions will no longer have preferential status. As a consequence, the dividend to all unsecured creditors is increased.

It remains to be seen whether the 'credit policy' of the Inland Revenue and HM Customs and Excise will become tougher if their preferential status is removed. Were either body to commence enforcement action more quickly against slow paying companies, this would almost certainly lead to more companies failing. However, this action would be contrary to the Government's stated policy of promoting 'corporate rescue'.

10 Are you at risk?

Many reasons have been put forward as to why a company fails. Historically a number of experts have compiled their own lists of warning signs, like the one in **Table 6** that may indicate possible difficulties arising in the future, and once a company's tally reaches a certain level, then that particular company is deemed to be 'at risk'.

10.1 Warning signs

The obvious warning signs are well known and have remained remarkably consistent since 1986, when the first edition of this book was written. For example, when a company becomes slow to settle its accounts and, when chased, the response is always that 'a cheque is in the post', this may mean that either the company's accounts department is hopelessly disorganised or the cash flow is giving cause for concern; perhaps the funds available are having to be spread thinly amongst creditors in an attempt to keep everyone happy. The finance director is often 'in meetings' and therefore unable to speak to creditors seeking payment.

These signs suggest that the company is already in the throes of financial crisis and is struggling to keep going. It is probably right up to, or even over the limit of, its bank facilities and therefore has little, if any, room for manoeuvre. However, it is rare that this state of affairs has arisen suddenly: the process of failure usually takes months, perhaps years, and during this time signs are normally apparent to the experienced observer, although not necessarily to the directors who are closely involved in the daily round.

It is essential therefore that the directors, or the credit controller, should be able to recognise the danger signs either in their own company or in those with which they trade, so that corrective or evasive action can be taken early enough to avoid potential disaster. There is no such thing as a 'fail safe' checklist, but the factors outlined below are some of those frequently put forward as being indicative that companies may be vulnerable.

Table 6: Early warning signals

- Rolls-Royce with personalised number plates
- Fountain in reception
- Flag-pole
- Recent move to unexpectedly luxurious offices
- Queen's award for industry (UK companies only)
- Whizz-kid vice chairman
- Unqualified or elderly accountant
- Auditors who 'grew with the company'
- Recent change of company bankers
- Market leader products
- Recent announcement of a technological breakthrough
- 'State of the art' computer system
- Unduly generous remuneration packages for directors

Almost invariably the company will be overtrading, financial control will be lax and accounts filed late. Dividends will be paid regularly despite declining profitability and rising borrowings, and, in a public company the announcement of results will be postponed.

This list is adapted from one suggested by Bill Mackey, then of chartered accountants Ernst & Young, at an accountants' conference and included in his chapter 'The receiver's view of the cause of failure' in *Managing for Profit* (McGraw-Hill, 1982). The list is illustrative only and obviously the presence of a flag-pole, for example, is not proof positive of imminent financial collapse. Nevertheless, it gives pointers which along with the other warning signs referred to in this chapter should put the observer on guard that all may not be as well as it appears. Impressive trappings may mask poor management or performance: what is the underlying business really worth?

10.1.1 The autocratic entrepreneur

It is a common view that success starts at the top: an ailing company is very often turned round and becomes profitable following the appointment of a new chief executive. Many small private companies, and even some quite large public ones, are run, apparently very successfully, by a dynamic entrepreneur who runs the company almost as a one-man band.

This entrepreneur is unlikely to be assisted by a strong management team – his personality will not permit it. However, should he lose interest after years of endeavour, or his judgement falter, he is unlikely to listen to other people, and his fellow directors may not be strong or able enough to control him and correct his mistakes. If no mistakes are made, then there will be no problem, but we are all human. Without a system of 'checks and balances' the company may be led in the wrong direction. In these circumstances the presence of strong independent or non-executive directors, as recommended by the Combined Code can be vital if a change of course is to be made.

There were a number of examples of colourful businessmen who built up substantial empires in the 1970s and 1980s and who were renowned for their autocratic leadership. However, with the change in the economic climate in the early 1990s many of these empires suffered spectacular collapses at the expense of their creditors and shareholders.

10.1.2 Lack of financial control

In many small private companies the accounting records are inadequate. Frequently the family company has grown up through the skills and energy of one person whose efforts have been directed towards sales and production. Overheads have been kept to a minimum – the finance function being regarded as an overhead.

There are no effective budgeting procedures, no monitoring of actual results against the forecasts, and there is inadequate husbanding of the company's resources, particularly cash. However good the company's products are, or successful the marketing strategy is, without an accurate 'score card', used intelligently to direct the business to its goal, the chief executive cannot be aware of the true direction in which the company is heading – the warning signs are simply not available.

Whilst this may be true for many smaller companies, some cynics would argue that many large and well-established companies have failed despite, or even because of, a plethora of rigorous financial controls and a welter of regular management information. Financial controls are only a means to an end. Regular and timely management information is only useful if the message conveyed is understood and acted upon effectively. If there is no finance director, or if there is one not strong enough to convince fellow directors that corrective action, however unpalatable, needs to be taken, then even the most sophisticated financial controls may serve little purpose.

10.1.3 Falling sales

At the risk of stating the obvious, however well managed and controlled a company is, if it does not sell its products in sufficient quantities to generate the desired level of income, it will fail to make a profit. The directors of a company whose market share is falling must find out why: is the product range outdated, or of poor quality? Is it being sold at the wrong price? A failure to carry out adequate market research initially or to react to subsequent changes in the market place is frequently indicative of weak management.

10.1.4 No sales!

Many companies of the dot.com variety exploded into the high-tech world of the twenty-first century with huge expectations of earning large revenues from changing the way business was transacted. Their directors convinced willing investors to part with many millions of pounds to enable the companies to develop ever more complicated and fanciful websites for their 'customers' to access. In some cases, it seemed the greater the monthly 'cash-burn' – the higher the share price, despite virtually all these companies being 'pre-revenue' i.e., they had no sales!

Gradually investors woke up – refused to part with any more cash – with the result that many companies failed. Those that survived realised that whatever the level of technology, at some point, and preferably sooner rather than later, a company's income stream must be greater than its expenditure!

10.1.5 The 'single product' company

A company which is mainly dependent upon either a single product or a single customer is always vulnerable to changes in technology or fashion which can lead to a rapid fall in sales. A takeover of the company's major customer may cut off future orders. If the directors have not made adequate contingency plans for these eventualities, they may be left with insufficient time after the event to put matters right. Similarly, if the company's future is dependent on a single major project, and that goes wrong, the consequences can be catastrophic.

10.1.6 Overtrading

Probably the most common mistake made by many companies, the smaller ones in particular, is that of overtrading – the business expands faster than the cash resources available. In an attempt to increase sales, margins may have been cut or sales made to customers with a higher credit risk, so that the rate of cash collection slows. Thus the company's working capital may become wholly tied up in stock and debtors, with the result that there is no money left to pay suppliers.

10.2 The new computer system

The installation of a new 'all singing, all dancing' computer system can be a complex and time-consuming task, which requires careful planning. To maximise the return on the investment in a new system, the computer programs, whether accounting, stock control, or distribution systems, should be properly integrated with each other. An adequate system of internal control must be in place to ensure that the information produced is accurate, up to date and relevant. Although the phrase 'garbage in means garbage out' is somewhat hackneyed, it remains very true! If the controls are not there, the management can be making strategic decisions based on incorrect data, with potentially disastrous results.

10.3 Financial ratios

Any decline in a company's financial health is normally apparent from an examination of a series of financial ratios: the traditional ones tend to highlight any deterioration in a company's liquidity. Examples are:

(a) the quick assets ratio: the ratio of cash, debtors and other readily realisable assets to current liabilities – ideally this should be 1:1;
(b) the current ratio: the ratio current assets bears to current liabilities. As current assets include less realisable assets, such as stock and work in progress, a ratio of about 1.5:1 would be regarded as perfectly reasonable.

In recent years more sophisticated ratios such as 'Z' and 'A' scores have been devised which attempt to take account of non-financial as well as financial factors. The reader is referred to other texts listed in the bibliography for further discussion of those alternative methods. Although the methods may differ, there is one point upon which all would agree: no single ratio or method should be relied upon in isolation, but if the same conclusion can be drawn from a number taken together, action is probably necessary.

The astute credit controller will probably calculate these and other ratios from the accounts of the company's major customers when assessing their credit-worthiness.

10.4 The benefit of hindsight

Prior to 1990 relatively little research, outside the academic world, had been undertaken into the causes of companies failing. During the last ten years, the Association of Business Recovery Professionals, known as 'R3' (formerly SPI) has conducted regular surveys of its membership requesting information about companies that were either active, or still trading at the time of their insolvency. One of the main objectives of these surveys is to provide an overview of the reasons why businesses fail.

The conclusions that can be drawn from these surveys vary to some extent, according to the stage in the economic cycle at the time the survey was undertaken, but the most common factors contributing to failure which seem to recur regularly are listed below.

10.4.1 Size

New businesses are the most likely to fail – figures from the Federation of Small Businesses indicate that 25 per cent of all businesses fail within three years of start up. R3's own figures show that more than two out of five of all business failures occur in businesses less than four years old. The R3 surveys clearly show that small companies are most at risk – in the ninth survey covering the year to June 1999, 88 per cent of the failed companies reported on had turnover of less than £5 million. In the previous survey covering the year to June 1997, the corresponding figure was 85 per cent.

If company size is determined by the number of employees, in each survey during the last six years the surveys recorded that between 75 and 85 per cent of each year's company failures had fewer than 15 employees.

10.4.2 Loss of market

Loss of market in a time of economic growth, tends to be a specific sector-related issue. For example, in the R3 survey carried out in 1999, loss of market is more of an issue for companies in the manufacturing, retailing and transport/communication sectors, than for those in the construction, finance and business services, and hotel and catering sectors. Nevertheless, it can occur for a variety of reasons, which arguably should have been identified by management before the effect on the company became terminal. Examples are:

- product obsolescence;
- intense competition in a mature market;
- price wars;
- loss of a major customer; and
- currency fluctuations.

What is rather more worrying is that many company directors do not appear to learn from past mistakes as nearly one in two cases in the 1999 survey, as opposed to one in three in the survey two years earlier, had experienced financial difficulties previously.

10.4.3 Management failure

Poor management has been consistently cited as a major factor in all the R3 surveys, where the reasons quoted for failure include:

- over-optimism when planning and budgeting;
- imprudent accounting policies;

- inadequate accounting and management information;
- product failure; and
- over gearing.

In times of low inflation, when margins in all sectors are often squeezed, the contrast between the well run and the poorly managed business becomes even more stark.

Insufficient equity and working capital are frequently quoted as the primary cause of failure, particularly in the case of smaller companies. Would-be entrepreneurs frequently underestimate the amount of capital required to finance the launch of a new enterprise in today's competitive environment. Nonetheless, control of working capital and cash flow management are the responsibility of the directors and hence external professional assistance must be obtained if the company does not have the necessary skills in-house.

10.4.4 Further education

These findings appear to support the contention that only a relatively small percentage of the directors of owner managed receive adequate training in running a business effectively, and hence the programme of formal training for company directors run by the Institute of Directors since 2000 should be encouraged.

A more detailed explanation of the lessons that can be learnt from other peoples' mistakes and the steps that directors should take in order to avoid going down the same path are contained in a booklet published by R3 entitled *The Ostrich's Guide to Business Survival.*

10.5 The minority view

If a director finds himself or herself to be in a dissenting minority on the board in a situation when there are doubts about the financial viability of the company, what steps can that director take to protect himself if his colleagues will not recognise that there may be a problem? Immediate resignation may not be sufficient, as if the company does fail subsequently, the conduct of all those who have been directors within the previous three years will be reviewed. In these circumstances the following steps should be taken by the individual director concerned prior to possible resignation:

(a) the director's concern should be formally tabled at the next board meeting, together with wherever possible, recommendations for action to be taken to correct or identify the problem;
(b) if appropriate, recommend that the board obtains professional advice, which could be from either the company's auditors or solicitors;

(c) if the board is unwilling to do this, the dissenting director's opinion must be formally recorded in the minutes of the meeting. If necessary, the director should seek his own professional advice, which is independent from the company's advisers. If still no progress is made then the director should convene a board meeting specifically to consider his concerns. If this does not lead to appropriate corrective action being taken, the director will have no alternative other than to resign but at least he has attempted, albeit unsuccessfully, to alert the board to the company's problems, and therefore cannot be accused subsequently of failing to act once aware of the company's financial position.

11 Conclusion

The efficient management of a company has many different facets, and therefore a team is needed to provide the relevant skills required. The talents of individuals need to be used to their best advantage and directed towards the common goal. In a small company the team may include part-time directors or the company's professional advisers. As the company grows, more expertise may be needed in-house and be involved in day-to-day management.

Directors can be jointly and severally liable for the actions of their board colleagues; ignorance of the offending transactions or circumstances may no longer be an adequate defence. So all directors, of whatever discipline, should be regularly advised of their company's financial and environmental position and ensure that they appreciate the significance of the information they are given. If in doubt, it is essential and in their own interests that independent advice is sought.

The obligations and responsibilities imposed on directors, not only by the Companies and Insolvency Acts, but increasingly by a welter of other legislation, much of which is derived from European directives, can be onerous and individuals should be aware of the responsibilities they assume when accepting a directorship. The law is intended to protect the public by penalising the relatively small number of directors who have acted irresponsibly and incompetently, without regard to their obligations to the parties with whom they deal.

Nevertheless, the courts do now expect a higher standard of care and skill by directors in the execution of their duties. It is hoped that a wider realisation that directors can and do suffer personal liability either for debts incurred or for offences committed by the company whilst under their control will encourage those directors who need encouragement to carry out their duties and functions more responsibly. If all else fails the courts will act, both to protect the public and to deter other directors from acting irresponsibly, by prohibiting delinquent directors from repeating their misdemeanours on future occasions.

Conclusion

Although the penalties to be incurred by delinquent directors are now more severe, the requirements of the legislation over, say, the maintenance of accounting records, the preparation of annual accounts or the duties owed to suppliers, are no more than would be expected for any well run and organised business, whether incorporated or not. However, in recent years, those responsible for representing the interests of the business community have complained vociferously about the ever growing burden that increasingly complex legislation and regulation places on small companies in particular. Even if only a fair proportion of the Company Law Review Group's proposals become law, the office of director will undoubtedly become more risky. Therefore a statutory statement of directors' duties, as proposed by the Review Group which both clarifies and simplifies their duties and obligations so that all involved in company management have a clear understanding as to what is expected of them, would be very welcome.

And whilst the Review Group's proposals to strengthen sanctions against errant directors where appropriate are laudable, when considering the relevant legislation, Parliament must ensure that the requirement to penalise those directors who fail to fulfil properly the obligations and responsibilities they take on when becoming a director, is balanced with the benefits to the business community of encouraging potentially successful entrepreneurs to become company directors. The directors of well-managed companies who act honestly at all times, carrying out their duties conscientiously with due skill and care must continue to be able to do so free of a fear of personal retribution should the occasional mistake be made.

Appendix Summary and references

This appendix contains:

- a summary of the content of 'Directors – responsibilities and liabilities' and page references;
- references to the Companies Act 1985 (as amended by the Companies Act 1989) (CA), the Companies Act 1989 (CA 1989), the Insolvency Act 1986 (IA), and the Company Directors Disqualification Act 1986 (DA), using the abbreviations as indicated in brackets. All other references are set out in full;
- references to case law together with a brief explanation of the relevance of the decisions made.

COMPANIES AND DIRECTORS

Directors – responsibilities and liabilities		Statute/case law	
Item	Page Ref	Item	Ref
1 Companies **Why a company?** – confers continuity and life on business as separate legal entity – shareholders own company – use of profits – director's liability – ideal vehicle for expansion	5	The company cannot litigate 'in person' and must be represented by a solicitor/barrister unless the court permits an unqualified person to act on the company's behalf	*Kinnell & Co v Harding* [1918] 1 KB 405
What sort of company? – private limited – public limited – takes on own debts – ownership separate from liability	5	Types of company	CA 1 (2), 11, 118
Incorporation – registration	6		
Formation – off the shelf companies – procedure less expensive but seek professional advice before acting	6	If you propose to acquire an off the shelf company for the purpose of carrying out an agreement, a minimal acknowledgement by the company of the agreement renders it liable after you become a director	*Phonogram v Lane* [1981] 3 All ER 182

COMPANIES AND DIRECTORS

Directors – responsibilities and liabilities		Statute/case law	
Item	Page Ref	Item	Ref
Publicity – filing at Companies House – compliance with company legislation – unlimited liability and its consequences	6	Filing with Registrar	CA 242
Company names – exclusions – where name must appear – non–compliance with requirements is an offence	7	company names Display of company's name	CA 25, 26 CA 348–51
Assets and liabilities – transfer agreement on incorporation – seek professional advice on tax and legal aspects	7		
Advantages and disadvantages of incorporation – limited liability entails increased disclosure and accountability – purpose of legislation is to protect third parties	8		
Finance – advantages when a company borrows money – tax advantages under the Enterprise Investment Scheme	8		

COMPANIES AND DIRECTORS

Directors – responsibilities and liabilities		Statute/case law	
Item	Page Ref	Item	Ref
Tax – income and corporation tax: rates and assessment – directors on PAYE system – treatment of benefits in kind, loans, credit facilities – need to obtain professional advice	9		Finance Acts
Retirement benefits – advantages of approved company schemes	11		
National Insurance contributions – higher payments and benefits	11		
Directors' liability – director acting responsibly not exposed to same risk as sole trader/partner – limited liability of shareholders; exceptions	12		

COMPANIES AND DIRECTORS

Directors – responsibilities and liabilities		Statute/case law	
Item	Page Ref	Item	Ref
Administration and records – records and financial information to be filed at Companies House	12	Company records	CA 352
Accounts and reports – accounts to comply with Companies Acts and filed – penalties for late filing – listed companies' heavier responsibilities; need to comply with the Listing Rules of the Financial Services Authority	12		CA 226 CA 242 CA 242A
The company's constitution *Memorandum of association* – the company's charter: • company name and address • objects • liability of members • initial nominal capital • names of subscribers	12 12	Memorandum of association	CA 2(1) The Companies (Tables A–F) Regulations 1985 (SI 1985/805) amended by SI 1985/1052

COMPANIES AND DIRECTORS

Directors – responsibilities and liabilities		Statute/case law	
Item	Page Ref	Item	Ref
Articles of association – the company's internal organisation: • company's relationship with shareholders • issue of share capital • appointment and powers of directors • procedures at meetings	14	Articles of association	CA 7, CA 8 The Companies (Tables A–F) Regulations 1985 (SI 1985/805) as amended
Single member companies	14	Single member companies	CA 1(3A)
Electronic communication – specified documents can be filed at Companies House electronically	14		CA (Electronic communications) Order (2000) (SI 2000/3373)
Limited Liability Partnerships – LLP has its own legal personality separate from its members. – registration process similar to a limited company	14		Limited Liability Partnerships Act 2000
Liabilities of LLP members – not joint and several for actions of other members. – no personal liability for debts of LLP.	15		
The downside of incorporation – same duty as private limited company to: – file information at Companies House	15		

COMPANIES AND DIRECTORS

Directors – responsibilities and liabilities		Statute/case law	
Item	Page Ref	Item	Ref
The downside of incorporation contd. – prepare and file audited accounts – maintain proper accounting records – Corporate insolvency procedures apply			
2 Directors and their responsibilities – minimum requirements for private companies	17	Definition of director; determined by function rather than title	CA 741(1) (2) DA 6(3)
Who is a director? – anyone who acts as a director	17	Who is the director?	DA 6 CA 741(1) (2)
Who can be a director? – exclusions: • company secretary, if also sole director • undischarged bankrupts • those disqualified • company's auditor • anyone over 70, but note exceptions • unsound mind • absence over six months	17	Minimum number of directors: sole director/company secretary exclusion Company auditor not to be a director Age limit	CA 282 CA 283(4) CA 1989 Pt II CA 293–4 CA Table A Art 88
Appointment of directors – appointed by: • subscribers to memorandum • those named in articles	17	Appointment of directors Memorandum of Association	CA 292 CA 10, 13(5)

COMPANIES AND DIRECTORS

Directors – responsibilities and liabilities		Statute/case law	
Item	Page Ref	Item	Ref
Appointment of directors contd. • nomination at first meeting • by specific provision in articles – subsequent appointments in accordance with articles – the notice of appointment – notice of residential/ service address			Companies (particulars of usual resident-ial address) (Confidential-ity orders) regulations 2002
Retirement and removal – one-third retire per year – removal by majority vote	18	Removal and appeal Age 70 Loss of office compensation	CA 303–4 CA 293–4 CA 312 and 316
The board of directors • need to work collectively • delegation of powers	18		
Directors and meetings Shareholders' meetings	19		
The AGM – frequency – approves reports – elects directors – approves auditors and their fees – approves share issues and dividends – extraordinary general meetings • to approve changes to memorandum and articles, change of name, etc.	19	AGMs: notice required; quorums, resolutions, record of proceedings	CA 366 369–70 376–83

COMPANIES AND DIRECTORS

Directors – responsibilities and liabilities		Statute/case law	
Item	Page Ref	Item	Ref
The AGM contd. – dispensing with AGM (private company) – right of director to call a meeting – waiver on meetings – the board chairman – minutes of shareholders' meetings to be available for inspection			CA 252
Board meetings – co-equal responsibilities of directors – danger of dispensing with meetings – directors' powers to call meetings	20		
Minutes of meetings – recording of major decisions affecting company	20		
Part-time directors – non-executive – alternate – nominee – de facto – shadow	21	Note: references to the general duties of directors in statutes relate also to non-executive directors. Alternate directors 'De facto' director: undertakes functions which could properly be discharged only by a director Shadow directors: though not formally appointed directors they are treated as such in relation to specific matters in order to impose liabilities and prohibitions on them	CA 741(1) CA 741(2) (3) DA 22(5) IA 251

COMPANIES AND DIRECTORS

Directors – responsibilities and liabilities		Statute/case law	
Item	Page Ref	Item	Ref
Directors as employees – service contracts and their contents – need for legal advice – the five year excess – availability for inspection – loss of office compensation – 'controlling' directors	22	Contracts of service: requirements, exemptions, penalties, loss of office compensation Payment of directors	CA 312–16 318–19 344 343(8) CA 311
Directors' duties – compliance with CA and general law plus three primary duties: • fiduciary duties • to exercise skill and care • statutory obligations	24		
Directors and the company	24		
Fiduciary duty – act honestly, in good faith and in the best interests of the company – take proper care of assets – no profit at company's expense	24	Note: fiduciary duty is owed to the company only. Even directors appointed by shareholders must put company interest first. Directors are trustees of of company's money and property . . . . . . and must act bona fide and not enhance self–interest, e.g. by enlarging capital to dilute a majority holding of shares . . . . . . nor by trying to give some shareholders extra rights without consent given in general meeting	*Great Eastern Railway Co v Turner* (1872) LR 8 Ch App 149 *Howard Smith Ltd v Ampol Petroleum Ltd* [1974] 1 All ER 1126 *Hogg & Cramphorn Ltd* [1966] 3 All ER 420

COMPANIES AND DIRECTORS

Directors – responsibilities and liabilities		Statute/case law	
Item	Page Ref	Item	Ref
Fiduciary duty contd. – disclose interest in transactions – avoid conflict: personal *v* company interests – no use of company property for personal benefit		Declaration of interests and benefits Secret profits: any undisclosed profit or gain made by a director through the use of company property belongs to the company	CA 317 *Regal (Hastings) Ltd v Gulliver* [1942] 1 All ER 378
Directors as agents – director acts on behalf of company – examples where directors may be held personally liable	25	When entering into company transactions, a director acts as the company's agent, which imposes duties of loyalty and good faith To bind the company, a contract must be one which the company's representative would normally have authority to make in the ordinary course of business A director is personally liable if he or she orders goods without mentioning the company's name	*Great Eastern Railway Co v Turner* (1872) LR 8 Ch App 149 *The Raffaela* [1984] Lloyds Rep 02 *& UBAF v European American Banking Corp* [1984] 2 WLR 508 *John Wilkes (Footwear) Ltd v Lee International (Footwear) Ltd* [1985] BCLC 444

COMPANIES AND DIRECTORS

Directors – responsibilities and liabilities		Statute/case law	
Item	Page Ref	Item	Ref
Business contracts – directors to disclose all personal interests & interests of connected persons – connected persons defined – disclosure requirements	25	Connected persons and fair dealings. Exceptions to this rule are listed in CA Table A, Art 94	CA 36 to 36C CA 346
Substantial property transactions – conditions applying to directors and connected persons – penalties for infringing requirements	25	Property transactions: definition, exemptions, restrictions, contravention Duty on directors that the (company) property in their hands . . . must be applied for the specified purposes of the company	CA 320–22, 322A *Selangor United Rubber Estates Ltd v Craddock (No 3)* [1968] 1 WLR 1555, 1575 atp.

COMPANIES AND DIRECTORS

Directors – responsibilities and liabilities		Statute/case law	
Item	Page Ref	Item	Ref
Loans, credit arrangements and guarantees – conditions applying to company losses, guarantees and securities to directors	26	*Loans*: prohibitions exemptions (low value, intragroup, holding company, expenses advances, money lending companies, house purchase). Disclosure	CA 330–38 CA 232 & Sch 6
– public company loans		*Quasi-loans*: prohibitions, exemptions (low value, intragroup, holding company, expenses advances, lending companies). Disclosure	CA 330(3) 332, 333, 336, 337, 338 & Sch 6, Part 1
		Credit transactions: prohibitions, exemptions (low value, arm's length holding company, expenses funds). Disclosure	CA 330(4) 335(1) 335(2) 336, 337 CA 232 & Sch 6, Part 1
		Material transactions: disclosure, exemptions	CA Sch 6, Part 1
		Transactions with company officers: definition and disclosure	CA 233 & Sch 6, Parts II & III
		Recognised banks: disclosure register, shareholders' statements, exemptions	CA Sch 6 Part III CA 343(2) (4) (8), 344

COMPANIES AND DIRECTORS

Directors – responsibilities and liabilities		Statute/case law	
Item	Page Ref	Item	Ref
Share dealings – no restriction provided directors inform company – specific controlling legislation and Stock Exchange regulations	26	*Shares*: allotment prohibitions re options, duties re disclosures and directors' loss of capital Note: no improper use of inside information permitted	CA 80 320, 323–29 Criminal Justice Act 1993
Insider dealings – manipulation of price sensitive information for personal advantage forbidden	26		Criminal Justice Act 1993 Code of Market Conduct Financial Services and Markets Act 2000
Political donations and expenditure – shareholder approval required	27	Political donations and expenditure to be approved by shareholders, and disclosed in the Directors' Report	Political Parties Elections and Referendums Act 2000

COMPANIES AND DIRECTORS

Directors – responsibilities and liabilities		Statute/case law	
Item	Page Ref	Item	Ref
Skill and care – need to exercise requisite degree of skill and care – degree of expertise commensurate with professional standing – full–time devotion to job – non–executive directors to exercise independent judgement: no 'rubber stamping'! – no objective standard – reference to standard required by the Insolvency Act in relation to wrongful trading	27	*Degree of diligence*: the reasonable care an ordinary man might be expected to take in the circumstances on his own behalf Note: • duties re honesty and fair dealing for directors less onerous than professionals re negligence • errors of judgement do not necessarily involve liability • directors not experts unless employed as such • courts reluctant to question bona fide decisions	*Re Barings (No. 5)* [1999] 1 BCLC 433 *Norman v Theodore Goddard* (1991) BCLC 1028 *D'Jan of London Ltd* (1994) 1 BCLC 561
Delegation – need to delegate wisely – overall responsibility is not delegable	29	'It (is not) desirable for any tribunal . . . to formulate precise rules for the guidance . . . of business affairs' a director must inform himself sufficiently about a company's affairs to enable him to perform his functions	*Dovey & Metropolitan Bank Ltd v Cory* [1901] AC 477, 488 atp. *Re Barings (No. 5)* [1999] 1 BCLC 433
Statutory duties *Administrative duties* – obligations in Companies and Insolvency Acts – penalties for failing to comply – delegation of duties to professionals	30		

COMPANIES AND DIRECTORS

Directors – responsibilities and liabilities		Statute/case law	
Item	Page Ref	Item	Ref
Statutory books – records • registers: ○ members ○ debenture holders ○ directors/ secretaries ○ interests in company shares ○ charges ○ transfers & allotments • minutes of shareholders' meetings – filing requirements • changes to regular reference date • copies of shareholders' resolutions, memorandum & article changes, annual return and audited accounts	31	Registration and its consequences Company membership Register of offices, directors and secretaries Register of share interests Register of members Note: • Each director should ensure he or she has adequate information at meetings • Each director has the power to call a meeting	CA 10–20 CA 22–24 CA 287–89 CA 325–29 CA 352–62
The annual return – summarises information in statutory books plus changes – requirements for compilation – 'shuttle' service	32	Annual return	CA 363–65

COMPANIES AND DIRECTORS

Directors – responsibilities and liabilities		Statute/case law	
Item	Page Ref	Item	Ref
Duties towards employees – legislation applies to all employers – claims are against company not directors unless there is fraud or negligence – relevant legislation *Discrimination* • individuals can be liable for discriminatory acts *Health and Safety* • directors must ensure health and safety of all employees *Occupational pension schemes* • minimum funding requirement • pay employee contributions to scheme within 19 days of month end	32 32 34 35	Directors' duties to have regard for interests of employees . . . and applicability to shadow directors	CA 309 CA 309(3) Health and Safety at Work Act 1974 Discrimination Acts
Environmental responsibilities – potential criminal liability for both companies and directors – 'consent', 'connivance' or neglect of directors – civil liability for pollution and the cost of any remedial work – consider introducing an environmental management system – seek assistance from relevant environment law enforcing authority – policy disclosure requirements	36		Environmental Protection Act 1990 Water Resources Act 1991 Environment Act 1995

COMPANIES AND DIRECTORS

Directors – responsibilities and liabilities		Statute/case law	
Item	Page Ref	Item	Ref
3 *Directors and corporate governance* **The Cadbury code** – Board structure – role of non-executive directors – reporting and controls	41 41		
The Greenbury Code – disclosure of directors' remuneration	42		
The Hampel Report – endorsed Cadbury and Greenbury codes – board's primary responsibilities are to: • enhance the prosperity of the business • ensure the interests of different stakeholders are taken account of	42		
The Combined Code – sets out 17 principles of good governance	42	mandatory for fully listed companies	
The role of the non-executive director – function must be more than simply to monitor the executive directors – contribute as a team member • contribute to strategic development • improve formal board procedures • promote management changes • monitor compliance with best practice • confidant to chief executive	46		

COMPANIES AND DIRECTORS

Directors – responsibilities and liabilities		Statute/case law	
Item	Page Ref	Item	Ref
Independence will be compromised if the director: – has recently been employed by the company – is employed by a major customer or supplier – is related to the board or senior management – is retained as a professional adviser – is financially dependent upon the remuneration received	47		
Term of office – should be specific – may be relatively short	47		
Prospective appointments – establish shareholders' strategic objectives – assess the quality of management information – meet the other directors – visit company's key locations – determine the role expected	48		

DIRECTORS AND THE ACCOUNTS

Directors – responsibilities and liabilities		Statute/case law	
Item	Page Ref	Item	Ref
4 Directors and the accounts	51		
The annual accounts	51		
– The Companies Act requirements: • profit and loss account • balance sheet		Companies to keep accounting records	CA 221
		Requirement to prepare accounts	CA 226, 227
		Form and content of accounts	CA Sch 4, 4A
• the accounting reference period		Additional disclosure requirements	CA 231, 232 Sch 5, 6
		The accounting reference period	CA 223–5
– requirement for AGM approval		Directors' report and duty to deliver accounts	CA 234 CA 241–4
– requirements for public and private companies		Penalties for defective accounts	CA 245 245A, 245B 245C
		Period allowed for laying and delivery	CA 242
– modified forms of accounts • for dormant companies			CA 246, 247
• for small and medium-sized companies		Qualification for company as small or medium-sized	
– abridged accounts for shareholders		Group accounts of holding companies	CA 227–230 248–9
– for small and medium-sized groups		Further alternative accounts for small companies	CA Sch 8
– publication of accounts on company website		Directors responsible for integrity of the website	
– Group accounts • consolidation exemptions		Wide definition of subsidiary	

DIRECTORS AND THE ACCOUNTS

Directors – responsibilities and liabilities		Statute/case law	
Item	Page Ref	Item	Ref
The directors' report – principal business activities: material changes and developments – recommendations on distribution of dividends – directors' shareholdings, interests and new issues – professional advice needed – the role of the auditors – acknowledge directors' responsibility for the preparation of financial statements – corporate governance compliance – *Directors' Remuneration Report*	54 55	 Directors' shareholdings	CA 234 CA 234 Sch 7, Part I Directors' Remuneration Report Regulations 2002
The auditors – the requirement for audited accounts – need for professionally qualified auditors – exemption from audit	55	 Qualifications for appointment of auditors	 CA 1989 25 CA 249A
Appointing the auditors – initial and subsequent appointments	56	Annual appointment of auditors	CA 384–388A
The auditors' report – report to all shareholders – general procedure and requirements – auditors' right of access to books and meetings – directors' confirmation – compliance with corporate governance Code	56	Auditors' report Auditors' duties and powers Signing of accounts	CA 235 CA 237 CA 233

DIRECTORS AND THE ACCOUNTS

Directors – responsibilities and liabilities		Statute/case law	
Item	Page Ref	Item	Ref
Accounting records – why easy access to accurate accounting records is important – requirements: • daily cash receipts and payments • assets and liabilities – if goods involved: • stock statement • description of goods bought and sold (not retail trade) – records to be available for inspection	57		CA 221
Management accounts – the need for management accounts – can reduce audit costs – assistance from auditors on format – coverage – profitability – cash management – budgets and forecasts – benefits if further credit required – importance of knowing company's true financial position – regular review with external accountants or the auditors can reveal potential problems	57		

THE COMPANY LAW REVIEW

Directors – responsibilities and liabilities		Statute/case law	
Item	Page Ref	Item	Ref
5 *The Company Law Review*	61		
Overall objectives – to create a framework of company law that strikes a proper balance between different stakeholder groups	61		
Law relating to directors' conduct has 2 purposes – regulation of relationships between directors, their company and the shareholders – to serve the wider public interest			
Role of director – codification of body of case law into schedule of general principles to be incorporated into legislation	62		
Directors as employees – increased disclosure of directors' transactions with the company in the interests of greater transparency – service contracts generally to be for a maximum of one year	64		
Sanctions for directors failing to: – disclose information on personal transactions with the company – maintain proper accounting records; – provide information to the auditors	65		

THE COMPANY LAW REVIEW

Directors – responsibilities and liabilities		Statute/case law	
Item	Page Ref	Item	Ref
Company administration and governance *Shareholders and company formation* *Company accounts* The auditors	66 66 67 67		
The government's response – priority for company law – 'think small first'	68	Modernising Company Law – White Paper July 2002	
Directors' Duties – Primary role – promote success of the company for benefit of the shareholders – Codification of general duties to the company to replace principles in existing body of common law – Government generally agreed with Review Groups proposals except recommendation that directors' duties prior to possible insolvency should be codified	68		

DIRECTORS' LIABILITIES CIVIL CLAIMS

Directors – your responsibilities and liabilities		Statute/case law	
Item	Page Ref	Item	Ref
Company administration and governance – Companies' constitution to be a single document *Private Companies:* • No requirement to hold AGM unless shareholder requisition • No necessity to appoint a company secretary • 'Definition' for small company increased • Abbreviated accounts to be abolished	69 70		
6 *Directors' liabilities* Civil claims – personal liability arises only from: • breach of statutory or other duties, or fraud	73 73	Fines for company offences, e.g., failure to keep statutory accounts	CA 221–2
• dereliction of duty in personal injury claims, etc.			
– personal liability incurred for: • acting outside provisions of memorandum and articles		A director acting contrary to memorandum or articles cannot bind the company unless his or her action is subsequently ratified by the company in a general meeting	*Royal British Bank v Turquand* (1856) 6 E & B 327; (1843–60) All ER Rep. 435 CA 35, 35A, 35B
• placing orders without reference to the company		Personal liability, e.g., authorising loans, unlawful dividends	CA 330 341
• signing cheques, etc. not carrying company name		Company name not on cheques	CA 349(4)

DIRECTORS' LIABILITIES CIVIL CLAIMS

Directors – responsibilities and liabilities		Statute/case law	
Item	Page Ref	Item	Ref
Civil claims contd. – liability for misfeasance by, e.g., making secret profits – application to court for relief – courts can relieve directors of liability if found to have acted reasonably		Minority shareholders can sue directors if the majority are grossly negligent & thereby gain a profit – even though there is no fraud Powers of court to relieve responsibility	*Daniels v Daniels* [1978] 2 WLR 73 CA 727 *Customs & Excise v Hedon Alpha Ltd* [1981] 2 All ER 697
The company and the director – company instigates court action – not acting in company's best interests can incur penalties – action where there is unfair prejudice against minority shareholders – powers of the court – DTI investigation a last resort	74	Where a company has suffered wrong, the only proper plaintiff is the company itself, i.e., the majority shareholders A minority can sue if there is 'unfair' prejudice', but such action can be difficult	*Foss v Harbottle* (1843) 2 Hare 461 CA 459 *Rolled Steel Products (Holdings) Ltd v British Steel Corporation* [1985] 2 WLR 908
Directors and shareholders – duty not to deceive shareholders – the Theft Act and the Companies Act provisions	75	*Shares*: allotment, prohibitions re options; disclosures and directors' duties re loss of capital. Note: no improper use of inside information permitted	CA 80, 320 323–9 Criminal Justice Act 1993

DIRECTORS' LIABILITIES CIVIL CLAIMS

Directors – responsibilities and liabilities		Statute/case law	
Item	Page Ref	Item	Ref
Directors and groups of companies – define the authority of each group company board – group transactions must be commercially justifiable – the parent company board as shadow director	75		
Takeovers and mergers – protection of rights of shareholders on takeovers or mergers – Takeover Panel supervises code by sanctions	76	Duty to disclose takeovers *Listed companies*: requirements of directors & duties re takeover offer	CA 314–15 City Code on Takeovers & Mergers Listing Rules of the FSA
Share issues – directors personally liable to compensate for losses arising from: • untrue statements in prospectus • deceptive inducements to invest • investor protection in public companies	76	*Subscribers misled by company prospectus*: Criminal liability for untrue statements Inducements to invest	Listing Rules of the FSA
Directors and taxation – if company's failure to pay is wilful or dishonest, directors can be personally liable for: • VAT penalties due • unpaid PAYE deductions • unpaid NI contributions	77		VAT Act 1994 Income Tax (Employment) Regulations 1993

DIRECTORS' LIABILITIES CIVIL CLAIMS

Directors – responsibilities and liabilities		Statute/case law	
Item	Page Ref	Item	Ref
Civil liability *The Thomas Saunders Partnership v Harvey*	78	Although Mr. Harvey's company Cavco Environments Ltd was the supplier of the offending materials it had been liquidated and unable to compensate the plaintiffs in full. The director was ordered to pay the balance	1989 Queens Bench (unreported)
Re Williams v Natural Life Health Foods		Franchisee relied upon expertise and experience of managing director for franchiser in preparation of profit forecasts which proved to be substantially wrong. Upon appeal to the House of Lords the director was found not to be personally liable, as there had been no conduct by the director to suggest he accepted personal responsibility	(1997) BCC 605
Re D'Jan of London Limited		Director found liable to compensate company for a loss incurred by him, because he had failed to check the insurance proposal which rendered the policy invalid	(1993) BCC 646
Directors and unpaid creditors – IA has strengthened position of creditors making claims • wrongful trading – additional to fraudulent trading – and its implications		*Wrongful trading*: the Act does not require any proof of dishonesty or bad intention. Dishonesty can be inferred if credit is taken or extended where there is no reasonable prospect of debts being paid	IA 214 DA 10

DIRECTORS' LIABILITIES CIVIL CLAIMS

Directors – responsibilities and liabilities		Statute/case law	
Item	Page Ref	Item	Ref
Directors and unpaid creditors contd. – the director's defence; exclusion in cases of recklessness or incompetence – joint and several responsibilities of directors			
Criminal liability – misappropriation a long standing offence – negligence, dishonesty or involvement in fraud can incur personal liability for company debts plus fine/ imprisonment – offences under general law can lead to criminal proceedings – 'strict' liability, e.g., under Trade Descriptions Act; no requirements to prove intent to defraud – limited liability normally applies under the general law	80	*Criminal liability*: e.g., • breaches of loans • being director of 'phoenix' company • failure to make out a Statement of Affairs • applying a false trade description to goods. Dishonesty does not have to be proved	CA 330 342 IA 216 IA 22, 47, 99 Trade Descriptions Act (1968 & 1972) *Alec Norman Garages v Phillips* [1985] RTR 164
Corporate killing – Senior management must have detailed personal knowledge to be held personally liable – Possible change in law: • to allow companies to be prosecuted for collective management failure • Personal liability for negligent directors	81	Government consultation paper (May 2000) — Reforming the law on Involuntary Manslaughter	

DIRECTORS' LIABILITIES CIVIL CLAIMS

Directors – responsibilities and liabilities		Statute/case law	
Item	Page Ref	Item	Ref
Disqualification – Insolvency Act extends directors' exposure to risk	82	Powers of court re disqualification order	DA 1–9
Company Directors Disqualification Act – Offences under the Companies Act – conviction of offence re promotion, formation management or liquidation of company – trading with intent to defraud in a winding up – company fraud	83	Fraudulent trading: carrying out company affairs with intent to defraud creditors. It is not necessary for the creditor to prove there was no reasonable prospect of the creditors receiving payment. But courts are reluctant to pass on personal liability unless there has been a knowing, wilful or deliberate personal involvement	DA 2(1) *R v Grantham* [1984] 3 All ER 166 DA 4(1) *R v Cox & Hodges* (1982) 75 Cr App R 291 *White Horse Distillers v Gregson Associates* [1984] RPC 61
– persistent non–compliance with directors' statutory obligations		Failure to file documents	CA 297
Disqualification after DTI investigation	83		*Re Samuel Sherman plc* (1991) 1 WLR 1070

DIRECTORS' LIABILITIES CIVIL CLAIMS

Directors – responsibilities and liabilities		Statute/case law	
Item	Page Ref	Item	Ref
Company Directors Disqualification Act contd. *Insolvent companies*		Reporting duties of office holders	DA 7(3) (4)
– application procedures – disqualification automatic under certain circumstances		Application for disqualification order	DA 8
– application for order by Secretary of State/ Official Receiver following report on directors' conduct		Impact of disqualification order Timing of application	DA 15 DA 7(2)
– DA's guidelines to court on fitness of directors • any breach of fiduciary duty • any misappropriation of assets • degree of responsibility for company transactions at undervalue • failure to keep adequate accounting records		Guidelines for 'unfitness' Who is the director? Badge of unfitness Matters applicable Did director act correctly?	DA Sch 1 DA 6 DA 9 &Sch 1 DA Sch 1, Parts I & II IA 214(4)
– if company insolvent, court to assess responsibility for: • causes of insolvency ○ failure to supply goods/services already paid for ○ voidable transactions ○ failure to call creditors' meeting		NB: if liquidation cannot be avoided, director should: • seek meeting of board to ensure his intentions minuted • try to persuade board to seek advice Entrusting of functions Company doctors	 IA 214(5) DA 15(4)
– where fraud needs to be proved; exceptions – term of disqualification			

INSOLVENCY

Directors – responsibilities and liabilities		Statute/case law	
Item	Page Ref	Item	Ref
Acting while disqualified – Register of Disqualification Orders – joint and several liability for debts incurred during disqualification	85	Departmental functions The register	DA 7(4) DA 18
Disqualification and Competition Law – Directors may be liable for disqualification for breach of competition law	85	Enterprise Bill	
Trading under the same name	85		IA 216 East Africa Lines Limited [1997] 141 SJLB 160
7 *Insolvency* – Insolvency Act incorporates some of the recommendations of Cork Report	87	The Cork Report	Insolvency Law & Practice: Report of the Review Committee 1982 (Cmnd 8558)

INSOLVENCY

Directors – responsibilities and liabilities		Statute/case law	
Item	Page Ref	Item	Ref
Identifying problems *Accounts and records* – need for regular management accounts • provision against the unforeseen • credibility in customers' eyes • need for accurate records when company under financial pressure • basis of directors' decisions – basic requirements: • short–term profit forecasts • cash flow projections • likely outcome of re-organisation or re-financing	87		
Options and decisions – if there are cash flow problems, directors need to consider: • corrective action • raising additional equity/loan capital • sale or merger – if further trading not possible: • informal arrangement with creditors • insolvency procedures	88		

INSOLVENCY

Directors – responsibilities and liabilities		Statute/case law	
Item	Page Ref	Item	Ref
When is a company insolvent? – no specific legal definition: • company unable to pay its debts as they fall due, or • value of assets less than liabilities – but Act requires contingent and prospective liabilities to be taken into account – technical insolvency – implications for financial position of assessments on going concern and break up basis	88	Insolvency definition	DA 6(2) IA 123
Insolvency and directors – the temptation to continue to trade – need to take professional advice – directors can be liable if they • issue cheques without funds • dispose of assets at undervalue • permit suppliers to recover stock – difficulty of making objective decisions under pressure – why directors need to know more about insolvency procedures	89		

INSOLVENCY

Directors – responsibilities and liabilities		Statute/case law	
Item	Page Ref	Item	Ref
Cash management – Cashflow projection essential – Communicate with debtors and creditors – Manage creditor expectations	90		
The interests of the creditors – Directors to seek advice of licensed insolvency practitioner – Creditors' interests paramount	91		
Institute of Directors' Publications			
The present insolvency regime *Company Voluntary Arrangements* – Supervisor monitors company management – Moratorium for small companies	92		IA 1–7 Insolvency Act 2000
Receivership – when debenture issued, lender can usually enforce security by appointing an administrative receiver *The receiver* – function • acts as company agent • to realise assets – ranking of claims – receiver not empowered to deal with unsecured creditors' claims	93	Appointment of receiver Powers and duties of receiver	IA 33–34 IA 42–43 46–49

INSOLVENCY

Directors – responsibilities and liabilities		Statute/case law	
Item	Page Ref	Item	Ref
Directors and receivers – when receiver appointed, directors' powers suspended but they remain in office – receiver appraises financial position; directors to assist – receiver decides how best to realise assets – directors' other powers continue and they must prepare a Statement of Affairs	94	Statement of Affairs	IA 47
Administration – opportunity to initiate receivership procedures where no debenture issued – need for expert advice – criteria for court order: • company is insolvent • order will enable company to: ○ survive as going concern, or ○ come to arrangement with creditors, or ○ secure more advantageous realisation of assets	94	Administration orders: purpose, application, effect, who makes the order and timing	IA 8–11
The administrator – administrator's proposals to creditors	94		IA 23–25
Directors and administrators – Directors to submit Statement of Affairs & supply all information required	96	Powers and duties of administrators	IA 14–23 & Sch 1

INSOLVENCY

Directors – responsibilities and liabilities		Statute/case law	
Item	Page Ref	Item	Ref
The Enterprise Bill Principal changes proposed: – holders of newly created floating charges cannot appoint administrative receivers, subject to specific exceptions – secured creditor can apply to appoint own nominee as administrator – administrator's primary duty is to rescue the company, rather than the business – administration must be completed within one year – Crown's preferential status will be abolished – Proportion of floating charge monies to be ring-fenced for unsecured creditors	97		Enterprise Bill (as at July 2002) s245 Schedule 16 s246 s247
Liquidation – how liquidation is instigated – the need for directors to seek advice on whether to go into voluntary liquidation	99		
Directors' responsibilities prior to liquidation – company under directors' control until liquidator appointed – liquidator advises directors	100		

INSOLVENCY

Directors – responsibilities and liabilities		Statute/case law	
Item	Page Ref	Item	Ref
Statutory duties – liquidator can be appointed more quickly in a voluntary liquidation – duty of directors to act quickly	100		
Preserving the assets – prior to liquidator's appointment, directors can: • dispose of perishable goods • act to protect company's assets – need to consult with insolvency practitioner – need to decide on: • retaining employees • ensuring assets are secure • converting work in progress into finished goods • referring creditors' requests for retention of goods to liquidator • opening separate account for creditors • freezing bank account • making cash payments for goods/services	100	*Fraudulent preference*: cheques paid into an account after a company ceases trading may be fraudulent preference even if paid in under the 'genuine & reasonable' belief that the company's creditors will be paid 'within a short time'	*Matthews Ltd F.P. & C.H. (in Liquidation) Ltd* [1982] 2 WLR 495

INSOLVENCY

Directors – responsibilities and liabilities		Statute/case law	
Item	Page Ref	Item	Ref
Voluntary liquidation – how it is instigated – if company solvent, voluntary liquidation can be agreed by resolution; if insolvent, company can be placed in creditors' voluntary liquidation by an extraordinary resolution – liquidator usually appointed by shareholders – requirements for creditors' meeting • notification • verification and presentation of Statement of Affairs • appointment of chairman • procedures – fines for non-compliance	101	Voluntary liquidation Requirements for creditors' meetings Statement of affairs	IA 95–99, 105, 114, 166 IA 95–99, 105, 166 IA 131
Directors and liquidators – when liquidator appointed, directors' powers cease – directors to assist liquidator; penalties for non co–operation	102	Powers of directors under voluntary liquidation	IA 114
The liquidator – principal duties • possess company's property • realise assets for benefit of creditors • agree creditors' claims & distribute assets realised in rank order • investigate company's affairs and conduct of its officers	102	Appointment of liquidator General functions of liquidator	IA 135–140, 143 IA 135(4)

INSOLVENCY

Directors – responsibilities and liabilities		Statute/case law	
Item	Page Ref	Item	Ref
Reports on the conduct of the directors – liquidator submits report to Secretary of State on directors' conduct – format of report: • details of all directors • their position • remuneration • list of other directorships • details of other companies directors are associated with • any other relevant matters • summary of Statement of Affairs – application for a disqualification order is made by the Secretary of State	103	*Conduct of directors*: includes actions connected with insolvency Report on directors	DA 6(2) Insolvent Companies (Reports on Conduct of Directors) (No. 2) Rules 1986
Directors' personal guarantees – when personal guarantees can become liabilities	105	Personal guarantees given in relation to subscription/sale	*National House Building Corporation v Frazer* [1983] 1 All ER 1090

DISQUALIFICATION – THE LESSONS TO LEARN

Directors – responsibilities and liabilities		Statute/case law	
Item	Page Ref	Item	Ref
Bank guarantees – personal guarantee of bank overdraft, backed by charge on director's house – need to resist request for charges over personal assets – the advantages of a debenture agreement – validity of bank's fixed charge on book debts – circumstances when bank may release personal guarantees	105		Re Brumark Investments Ltd
Business leases – landlords often require directors to guarantee a company's obligations under a lease – procedures and dangers	106		
Hire purchase and leasing agreements – requirements of finance companies	*107*		
Insolvency and director disqualification *Primary purposes* – to protect the public – to encourage other directors to behave well	109		

DISQUALIFICATION – THE LESSONS TO LEARN

Directors – responsibilities and liabilities		Statute/case law	
Item	Page Ref	Item	Ref
The grounds for disqualification – Case law has identified • transgressions which warrant disqualification • appropriate period of disqualification • those individuals who should be disqualified	111		
Unfit Conduct – in a capitalist society we should be allowed one mistake • phoenix companies • arrears of crown debts • excessive remuneration • accounts and accounting records • misappropiation of assets • failure to co-operate with office holder • trading whilst insolvent	111	The judge in *Majestic Recording Studios Ltd* was not as generous as might be thought. The judgment was given on 25 March 1988 and accounts to 31 March 1987 had to be audited, and filed by 31 May 1988	*Re IRcon Fashions Ltd* *Re Stanford Services Ltd* *Re D F Limited* 1987 *Re Majestic Recording Studios Ltd* *Re Cladrose Limited*

DISQUALIFICATION – THE LESSONS TO LEARN

Directors – responsibilities and liabilities		Statute/case law	
Item	Page Ref	Item	Ref
Period of disqualification – Mitigating factors may include: • acting upon professional advice • employed qualified staff • regular management information • personal financial loss • failure due to external factors	114	Guidelines for seriousness of offences re period of disqualification. 2–15 years	*Re Sevenoaks Stationers (Retail) Limited*
De facto directors	116	Son had assumed the status of director	*Re Cargo Agency Ltd* *M O' Donnell & Sons (Huddersfield) Ltd*
Standard of competence – directors of an insolvent company may be disqualified if they are found to be unaware of directors' duties or have no commercial experience	116		*Re Ameron Limited (1997)* *Re City Investment Centres Ltd*
Professionally qualified director – high standard of skill and care required – inactivity no excuse for a nominee director	117		*SSTI v Solly* *SSTI v Vass & Anor*
Allocation of responsibility	119		*Re Austinsuite Furniture Ltd*

DISQUALIFICATION – THE LESSONS TO LEARN

Directors – responsibilities and liabilities		Statute/case law	
Item	Page Ref	Item	Ref
Delegation and supervision – the board and each director remain responsible for delegated functions and retain a residual duty of supervision and control	119		*Re Barings plc (No 5)*
Non–executive directors – required to be vigilant and aware of what is going on	121		*Re Continental Assurance Co. of London plc*
Company doctors – high degree of skill expected – Contractual terms of engagement by company to be clear	122	A consultant who is actively involved in the conduct of a company's business may be regarded as a *de facto* director	*Re Tasbian Limited (No. 3)*
Disqualification and leave to continue to act – Court has unfettered discretion to grant leave – protection of the public is paramount	123	Safeguards required by the court; difficulty in monitoring maintenance of safeguards	*Re Gibson Davies Limited*
Directors' disqualification and the public interest – ordinary commercial misjudgement is not sufficient to justify disqualification – mitigating factors • no dishonesty • personal financial loss • professional advice	124		*Re Bath Glass Ltd*

DISQUALIFICATION – THE LESSONS TO LEARN

Directors – responsibilities and liabilities		Statute/case law	
Item	Page Ref	Item	Ref
Carecraft and fast-track disqualification – disqualification by consent without a court hearing when the facts are agreed – Voluntary undertakings; acceptance at discretion of Secretary of State, if considered expedient in the public interest – effect of undertaking is the same as disqualification order	126		*Re Carecraft Construction Limited* IA 2000 IA 2000
Wrongful trading – director's knowledge not limited by documents available at the time – director's knowledge includes all matters 'they should have found out' – contribution by directors to the assets of a company in insolvent winding up equal to liabilities incurred from the date that company clearly insolvent – Husband and wife both guilty of wrongful trading, although wife had little involvement in company's affairs	127		*Produce Marketing Consortium Ltd* *Re Purpoint Limited* (unreported) IA 214 IA 214(4) DA 6 *Re Brian D Pierson (Contractors) Ltd*

ARE YOU AT RISK?

Directors – responsibilities and liabilities		Statute/case law	
Item	Page Ref	Item	Ref
Wrongful trading contd. – directors not found liable for wrongful trading:		– main director had died and so could not give evidence – all had extensive business experience – no personal gain – all were aware of what was going on and had not deceived creditors	*Sherborne Associates Limited*
9 Directors' unlimited liability – a case study	131		
10 Are you at risk? **Warning signs** – list of early warning signals – common warning signs are usually obvious to many, but not always to directors who are closely involved	137 137		
The autocratic entrepreneur – normally works without strong advisers, which can be dangerous if mistakes occur *Lack of financial control* – dangers of inadequate financial records, particularly in family companies, and lack of financial procedures – no warning signs available – even sophisticated controls worthless if ignored	138 139		

ARE YOU AT RISK?

Directors – responsibilities and liabilities		Statute/case law	
Item	Page Ref	Item	Ref
Falling sales – profit depends on selling products in sufficient quantities – need to examine reasons for falling sales	139		
The 'single product' company – vulnerable to change	140		
Overtrading – the business expands faster than cash resources available	140		
The new computer system – the system must be relevant to the company's needs – be properly integrated, with an adequate system of internal controls – be properly tested before going 'live', with adequate support to cope with initial teething troubles	140		
Financial ratios – examples: • quick assets • current ratio • more sophisticated ratios – reliance on several ratios recommended	141		

ARE YOU AT RISK?

Directors – responsibilities and liabilities		Statute/case law	
Item	Page Ref	Item	Ref
The benefit of hindsight – R3's surveys show that the most common factors contributing to failure are: • size – small companies most at risk • loss of market for product/services • management failure • inadequate financial resources	141		
The minority view – prior to resignation ensure that: • director's concern is formally minuted • seek independent advice • table action plan – if no consensus then submit resignation	143		

Index of cases

Alec Norman Garages v Phillips	(1985) RTR 164
Re Ameron Limited	(1997) Unreported
Re Austinsuite Furniture Limited	(1992) BCLC 1047
Re Bath Glass Limited	(1988) 4 BCC 130
Re Blackspur Group plc	(1997) BCC 235
Re Brian D Pierson (Contractors) Limited	(1999) BCC 26
Re Brumark Investments Limited	(2000) 1 BCLC 353
Re Carecraft Construction Limited	(1994) 1 WLR 172; (1993) BCC 336
Re Cargo Agency Limited	(1992) BCC 388
Re City Equitable Fire Insurance Co Ltd	(1925) 1 Ch 407
Re City Investment Centres Limited	(1992) BCLC 956
Re Cladrose Limited	(1990) BCC 11 (1990) BCLC 204
Re Continental Assurance Co of London plc	(1996) BCC 888
Custom & Excise v Hedon Alpha Limited	(1981) 2 All ER 697
Daniels v Daniels	(1978) Ch 406
Re Dawson Print Group Limited	(1987) 3 BCC 322
Re DF Limited (1987)	(1987)
Re D'Jan of London Limited	(1993) BCC 646 (1994) 1 BCLC 561

Phonogram v Lane	(1981) 3 All ER 182
Re Produce Marketing Consortium Limited	(1989) 5 BCC 569
Re Purpoint Limited	(1991) BCC 121
Re Queens Moat Hotels plc	Mr Registrar Jaques, unreported, 24/7/00
R v Cox & Hodges	(1983) BCLC 169
R v Grantham	(1984) BCLC 270 (CA)
Regal (Hastings) Limited v Gulliver	(1942) 1 All ER 378
Rolled Steel Products (Holdings) Limited v British Steel Corporation	(1985) 2 WLR 908
Re Rolus Properties Ltd and Another	(1988) 4 BCC 466
Royal British Bank v Turquand	(1856) 6 E & B 327 (1843–60) All ER Rep. 435
Re Samuel Sherman plc	(1991) 1 WLR 1070
Re Secretary of State for Trade and Industry v Solly	(1999) BCC 390
Selangor United Rubber Estates Limited v Craddock (No 3)	(1968) 1 WLR 1555
Re Sevenoaks Stationers (Retail) Limited	(1990) BCC 765
Re Sherborne Associates Limited	(1995) BCC 40
Re Standford Services Limited	(1987) 3 BCC 326
Re Tasbian Limited (No 3)	(1992) BCC 358
The Raffaela	(1984) 1 Lloyd's Rep 102
The Thomas Saunders Partnership v Harvey	(1990) Queens Bench 30 Con LR 103 9 Tr L 78
Re Times Graphic Systems Limited	Mr Registrar Jaques, unreported, 27/7/00

α No reference found

Bibliography

Companies and directors

Cadbury, A	Board Focus – *the Governance Debate: a current View of International Corporate Governance and the Responsibilities of Directors and Boards*, Egon Zehnder International 1997 *Final Report* (Hampel Report)
Davison, IH	*Is better corporate governance working?* ICAEW Centre for Business Performance, 2001
Financial Law Panel	*Joint Venture Companies – a practical guide to a director's duties, 2000. Operating subsidiaries – the organisation of director's responsibilities within a group*
Garratt, B	*The Fish Rots From the Head – the crisis in our Boardrooms: Developing the Crucial Skills of the Competent Director*, Harper Collins Business, 1996
Grundy, T	*The accountant as future chief executive* ABG Professional Information 2001
Institute of Directors	*The Company Director's guide – your duties, responsibilities and Liabilities Standards for the Board*
Secretary of State for Trade & Industry,	*Modernising Company Law* (HMSO July 2002)
Stiles, P	*Boards at work – Law directors view their roles and responsibilities* OYP 2001
The Company Law Review Steering Group	*Modern Company Law for a competitive economy* (HMSO 2001)
T Ricker RI	*Pocket Director* (*The Economist* in association with Profile Books, 2000)

Insolvency

Association of Business Recovery Professionals	*The Ostrich's Guide to Business Survival, (R3)* *Understanding Insolvency (R3)*
Sealy, LS	*Annotated Guide to the Insolvency Legislation*, CCH, 1994
Tolmie, F	"*Introduction to Corporate and Personal insolvency Law*" Sweet & Maxwell 1998

Index

Location references are to paragraph numbers. Table references are in italics.
Major location references are indicated by the use of bold type.
The Appendix and Bibliography are not covered.